Weapons of the Navy SEALS

FRED J. PUSHIES

MBI

First published in 2004 by MBI, an imprint of
MBI Publishing Company, Galtier Plaza, Suite 200,
380 Jackson Street, St. Paul, MN 55101-3885 USA

MBI titles are also available at discounts in bulk quantity
for industrial or sales-promotional use. For details write
to Special Sales Manager at Motorbooks International
Wholesalers & Distributors, Galtier Plaza, Suite 200,
380 Jackson Street, St. Paul, MN 55101-3885 USA.

ISBN 0-7603-1790-9

Edited by Steve Gansen
Designed by Mandy Iverson

Printed in Hong Kong

On the front cover: A Navy SEAL braves the surf as he transitions from the ocean to the shoreline. He keeps the mouthpiece of his lung automatic rebreather (LAR-V) in place in case he is engaged by the enemy and must evade back into the water.

On the back cover: U.S. Navy SEALs emerge from the ocean and through the raging surf. The SEALs, who derive their name from their operational elements—**SE**a, **A**ir, and **L**and—are the U.S. Navy's contribution to the U.S. Special Operations Command (SOCOM). This pair of SEALs from SEAL Team 3 is equipped with M4 carbines, a shortened version of the M16A1 rifle.

On the frontispiece: The AK-47 and AK-M 51x39mm assault rifle is the preferred weapon of many terrorists, and one of the most proliferated weapons in the world. For this reason, SEALs not only know how to deal with them as a threat but how to operate and employ them should the need arise. This assault rifle can be fired in semiautomatic or full-auto modes. It fires 7.62mm x 39mm rounds from a double-stacked 30-round magazine. The weapon is 34.2 inches long and weighs 9 pounds, 8 ounces. *Defense Visual Information Center*

On the title page: Members of SBT22 move through the waterways to extract a patrol during a training exercise.

About the author: Fred J. Pushies has spent the last 16 years in the company of each of the units assigned to United States Special Operations Command (SOCOM). He has skimmed across the waves with the SEALs in a Mark V, flown at treetop level with the 160th Special Operations Aviation Regiment, and crunched through the brush with Force Recon Marines. His integrity and insight are evident in his previous works, *Special Ops: America's Elite Forces in 21st Century Combat, U.S. Air Force Special Ops, U.S. Army Special Forces,* and *Marine Force Recon.*

Contents

Acknowledgments

I first wish to convey my personal thanks to the Almighty God, who has endowed our great nation with the liberty and freedom; which we, as Americans, cherish. May this great gift, which has been paid for with the sacrifices of many lives, never be taken for granted. To my family for their continued support in my projects. And to Steve Gansen, my editor at MBI Publishing Company.

U.S. Special Operations Command Public Affairs Office, Chet Justice; Naval Special Warfare Command Public Affairs Office, Coronado, Patricia O'Connor and Senior Chief A. Mansfield; Special Warfare Group Two Public Affairs Office, Lieutenant John Perkins; U.S. Navy Public Affairs Office, New York, Lieutenant Karen Sandoz; UDT-SEAL Association, Bob Rieve; Special Boat Team 22, Petty Officer First Class Lee Estes (Ret.); Seawolves Association, Frank Gale, President, and Bill Rutledge, Roll of Honor coordinator; United States Naval Institute Photo Archive, Sarah Moreland; National Archives, JoAnn Bromley.

I would like to thank the following companies and individuals for their invaluable assistance to this book: Black Hawk Industries, Mike Noel, President, and Scott Berube; WileyX, Myles Freeman, Executive Vice President, Sales; Bolle', David Cain; Boston Whaler, Kelly Webb; Columbia Rope, Division Manager Richard Sleight; Specialized Technical Services, Rob Stephens; Armor Holdings, Cheryl Munn; Knight's Armament Company; New Eagle International; Mustang Survival, Steve Chambers; Aimpoint, Mike Kingston; EOTech, Van Donahue, Vice President, Mike Curlett, Technical Sales Support, and Rod Coons and John Long, Directors of Sales (East/West); Thales Communications, Tammy Turner, Marketing Communications Manager; Specialized Technical Services; Insight Technology, Chris Feinauer; Heckler & Koch; Litton; High Speed Gear, Gene Higdon; Trijicon; Benelli USA, Debbie Hume; Motorola; Sonetronics; Raytheon; McMillion Brothers; and many others who wish to remain behind the scenes.

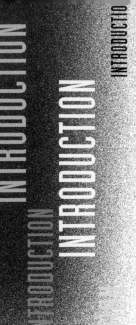

Introduction

When you mention the name Navy SEALs, it evokes many thoughts and perceptions. Some are ambiguous, but others are accurate. Whether it is through Hollywood's depiction in the cinema, or the numerous documentaries that have surfaced on the History Channel, these waterborne commandos have gained a popularity that has made them our nation's new folk heroes. The coonskin cap, the Stetson, and the Green Beret have given way to the floppy hat and flippers of the Navy SEALs in the heritage of our country and the legacy of the United States military.

Although their exploits during the Vietnam War were renowned, after the conflict the teams were downsized, and they entered into the secret world of unconventional warfare. They would surface from obscurity on occasion, but the Navy still held them under tight security. It has not been that long since the SEALs have come into the public eye. It was little more than a decade ago that the SEAL teams were classified and dealt with accordingly. While doing some research on special operations in the late 1980s, I called the Naval Special Warfare Group public affairs office. The gentleman on the other end of the line replied, "Navy SEALs do not exist; we do not talk about them." *Click.* The phone went silent.

"We have come farther than that," relates Patricia O'Connor, Assistant Deputy for Public Affairs. Today, the phone rings off the hook and email floods the computers at the public affairs office of the Naval Special Warfare Command—NavSpecWarCom—in Coronado, California. "Not a day goes by without a dozen calls from journalists, authors, movie writers, and the like, seeking out the SEALs." It is said that "the cost of peace is eternal vigilance," and the public affairs folks on the Silver Strand are committed to this cause as they stand at the portals of SEAL information, wielding the public affairs craft with as much aplomb as their charges.

It would not be until the victory in Desert Storm that the SEALs would step from the shadows and become open to the media and the public. Although they are still camera shy for a number of reasons, this elite band of frogmen-commandos discovered that there were some advantages in dealing with the public. While their missions are still of a sensitive nature, and many remain classified to this day, they also embraced a newfound relationship with the American public. Whether it is Fleet Week in New York harbor, or Independence Day in Coronado, you are likely to see a SEAL team displaying its gear or demonstrating its capabilities.

The weapons and equipment of the SEALs are as varied as the men themselves. On the West Coast you may see a collection of gear from suppliers such as Special Operations Equipment or the Tactical Tailor. On the East Coast you will note labels from Black Hawk, Eagle, or London Bridge equipment, or perhaps a collection of each stowed in kit bags and conex shipping containers bound for undisclosed locations. Members of the teams are given wide latitude with respect to the equipment they carry, and for this reason they are issued purchase cards. If they see an item that is useful, they can buy it on the spot. There is no red tape, no bureaucratic bean counters. If it is mission-essential, it is acquired, and no questions are asked.

Contrary to sales and marketing advertisements, there is *no* established "SEAL" watch, knife, boot, socks, gloves, etc. If two operators happen to purchase the same timepiece it is immediately marketed as "the official SEAL watch." In reality, the teams and operators obtain what works for them at a given mission or operation. Team 1 might choose a Ka-Bar knife, whereas Team 4 might prefer a SOG knife, or vice versa—or something entirely different.

The purpose of this book is to show some of the tools of the trade, and to share these tools with the supporters and admirers of these waterborne warriors. It is also to honor these men, who battle behind the lines and under the sea, at times making the ultimate sacrifice for freedom and their country.

Regarding the issue of operational security (OPSEC) Senior Chief A. Mansfield of NavSpecWarCom raised his concern that such a project could be advantageous to their adversaries and voiced a concern for his team-

mates in a manner consistent with his rank, which is to say forcefully. Thus a paradox is created for the author: How does one convey such information to the reader while maintaining the necessary secrecy? To assuage these concerns, I discussed the issue with a number of operators, and was drawn to the following premise, else this book would conclude here, at the introduction.

It is not the weapon that a man carries, it is not the knife he has slung on his belt. Neither is it the gadgets or gizmos of high-tech wizardry he carries in his tactical vest or load-bearing equipment that sets him apart from his compatriots and head-and-shoulders above his adversaries. No, these are mere tools in his hands. What sets the U.S. Navy SEAL apart is not the equipment; it is the fire in his gut, the tenacity in his spirit, and the ingrained certainty instilled into his warrior soul from evolution to evolution that he is a SEAL and he is the best. As part of a team, he is unstoppable, invincible. Following a UDT-SEAL reunion, I received a T-shirt from a member of SEAL Team 2 that reads "To find us, you've got to be smart. To catch us, you've got to be fast. To beat us, you've got to be kidding!"

This is a unit that needs no further introduction; its heritage and missions are legendary. It has been my pleasure and privilege to spend time in the surf, in the desert, and on the boats with members of both the West Coast and East Coast teams. *HOO-YAH!*

HISTORY

During a special message to the joint session of Congress on May 25, 1961, President John F. Kennedy stated, "I am directing the Secretary of Defense to expand rapidly and substantially, in cooperation with our Allies, the orientation of existing forces for the conduct of non-nuclear war, paramilitary operations, and sub-limited or unconventional wars. In addition, our special forces and unconventional warfare units will be increased and reoriented. Throughout the services new emphasis must be placed on the special skills and languages which are required to work with local populations."

Such an unconventional Army unit already existed in the Special Forces, or Green Berets, and the Air Force had its Air Commandos, and both units had established lineages. The President was a military scholar with more than a casual interest in counterinsurgency. He had been a PT-boat skipper during World War II, and he wanted to know what capabilities *his* branch of the service, the Navy, could bring to the special warfare arena. Following the direction of the Commander-in-Chief, on January 1, 1962, the Navy created the U.S. Navy SEALs and commissioned SEAL Team 1 on the West Coast and SEAL Team 2 on the East Coast.

The SEALs had a rich heritage to draw from, the underwater demolitions teams (UDTs) of World War II, and the naval combat demolition units (NCDUs). These elite frogmen were all volunteers and performed their perilous missions equipped with pencil and slate, while armed with only a Ka-Bar knife; they had earned the title "naked warriors." Their mission was to carry out hydrographic reconnaissance and clear natural or man-made obstacles ahead of amphibious assaults. To address the need for such a unit, on August 15, 1942, volunteers from the Army and Navy were brought together at the Amphibious Training Base, Little Creek, Virginia, for training as amphibious scouts and raiders. The scouts-and-raiders mission would be to reconnoiter beach landing sites, stay in position before the landing, and guide assault units to the landing site.

Above: **Following in the fin-strokes of their predecessors, the Underwater Demolition Teams, today's Navy SEALs carry on the tradition established by those "Naked Warriors" of World War II. Although their weapons and equipment have improved over the years, it is still their determination, courage, and teamwork that meld SEALs into the lethal combatants of today's Naval Special Warfare community. Here they practice cast-and-recovery operations from a patrol boat and the venerable IBS (inflatable boat small).**
Defense Visual Information Center

Left: **"Mission Complete. Request Exfil." A SEAL platoon leader instructs his radioman to advise the extraction helicopter that they are ready. They have "thrown smoke" to identify their position for the in-bound helicopter. The SEALs were first organized in 1962 to conduct unconventional warfare and counter-guerrilla operations during the Vietnam War. More than 40 years later, they stand as the Navy's premiere warriors among the U.S. Special Operation Forces.**

The first group was commissioned in October 1942, and it saw combat a month later in Operation Torch, the allied landings on the North Africa coast. Scouts and Raiders would also provide support for the Allied landings in Sicily, Salerno, Anzio, Normandy, and southern France. Among this group was Phil H. Bucklew, who would come to be referred to as the "Father of Naval Special Warfare."

Special Service Unit #1 (SSU#1) was the code name for a second group of Scouts and Raiders, which was formed on July 7, 1943, as a joint Army/Navy unit. Its first mission, in September 1943, was on New Guinea, and subsequent operations were at Gasmata, Arawe, Cape Gloucester, and others points along the coast of New Britain. All of these missions were carried out without the loss of any scouts and raiders. Then SSU#1 was summarily separated, and the naval personnel were assigned to 7th Amphibious Scouts. During the remainder of the Pacific War, the scouts of the 7th participated in more than forty landings.

A third Scout and Raider unit operated in China, where it conducted guerrilla-type missions and operated covertly against the Japanese.

The underwater demolitions teams (UDTS) obtained their "baptism by fire" on Operation Flintlock in the Marshall Islands on January 31, 1944. Ultimately, 34 UDT teams were created, and they were active throughout the Pacific Theater in all major amphibious landing operations, including Eniwetok, Saipan, Guam, Tinian, Angaur, Ulithi, Pelilui, Leyte, Lingayen Gulf, Zambales, Iwo Jima, Okinawa, Labuan, and Brunei Bay. Although they made no lasting trails through the water, the men of the UDTs made their mark in the world of unconventional warfare and set the benchmark for those who would follow.

On the other side of the world, the plan for the invasion of northwestern Europe called for a massive armada of ships and men to cross the English Channel and assault the French coastline. Intelligence gathering indicated that the Germans were emplacing a network of widespread underwater obstacles on the beaches at Normandy. The landing sites would have to be reconnoitered and details must be brought back to General Dwight Eisenhower and his staff.

On May 7, 1943, Lieutenant Commander Draper L. Kauffman was instructed to establish a school that would train people to remove obstacles on an enemy-held beach prior to an invasion. On June 6, 1943, a year before the D-Day invasion, Kaufman set up the Naval Combat Demolition Unit training base at Fort Pierce, Florida. On June 6, 1944, Operation Overlord commenced; the invasion of France was underway, and the men of the NCDUs carried out their tasks. On Omaha Beach they opened eight full gaps and two partial gaps in the German defenses. At Utah Beach they cleared 700 yards of beach in two hours, and went on to clear another 900 yards by the afternoon.

In addition to the UDTs and NCDUs, naval personnel served with the Office of Strategic Service, (OSS) as "operational swimmers" in the OSS maritime unit. These underwater warriors, all of them volunteers, would serve as the prototypes of the future SEALs by forging new techniques such as pioneering the use of swim fins, face masks, closed-circuit diving gear, submersibles, combat swimming, and limpet mines. Members of the OSS maritime unit formed part of UDT-1 in July 1944, and conducted the very first UDT/submarine operation from the USS *Burrfish* in the Caroline Islands.

The post-World War II demobilization dynamically reduced the UDTs down to two teams on each coast, each with a complement of 7 officers and 45 enlisted men. But the respite for the teams would not be long, for on June 25, 1950, the North Korean Army invaded South Korea, signaling the beginning of the Korean War.

At the onset of the new war, UDT 3 had a complement of just 11 officers and men, but in due course the unit was expanded to three teams with a total strength of 300.

On September 15, 1950, members of the UDTs supported the amphibious landing at Inchon, South Korea. UDT-1 provided personnel who preceded the landing craft to scout and identify the mud flats and low points in the channel. These "frogmen" also searched for mines and even cleared fouled propellers. During the Marine landing, four UDT personnel served as guides for the landing force.

The first use of a closed-circuit "aqualung" in combat operations was in October 1950 when UDTs supported mine-clearing operations in Wonsan Harbor. Here the team members located and marked mines for minesweepers.

The Korean War saw the UDTs move inland, beyond the surf zone. The North Koreans were being supplied via highways and rail lines in close proximity to the shoreline. Vice Admiral Turner C. Joy, commander of naval forces in the Far East, formulated a strategy to harass the enemy by disrupting his supply lines. The plan called for small amphibious teams to infiltrate from the sea to conduct raids against the North's supply routes. The first such raid conducted by the UDT men was against Yosu, on the south coast forty-five miles behind enemy lines. Yosu was a vital seaport consisting of a railhead, three bridges, and a tunnel. As the UDT men approached their insertion point in small, inflatable rubber boats in the blackness of night, they came under fire and were forced to abort the raid.

Although the mission had not been successful, it did provide lessons. Future raiding parties were augmented with Marines for added fire power. This combination of UDT and USMC provided a "commando" unit that would be successful in future operations.

For the balance of the Korean War, UDTs conducted beach and river reconnaissance, and infiltrated guerrillas behind the lines from the sea. These highly trained and motivated "frogmen/commandos" also successfully conducted numerous demolition raids on railroad tunnels and bridges along the Korean coast.

As the hot war evolved into the Cold War, the frogmen underwent another metamorphosis. The Navy's response to President Kennedy's request for the military to develop an unconventional warfare (UW) capability was the establishment of SEAL Teams 1 and 2 in January 1962. Drawing entirely from UDTs, these two new teams were given their mission to carry out counterguerilla warfare and clandestine operations in maritime (blue water) and riverine (brown water) environments.

The term SEAL is an acronym for the methods of insertion as well as environments in which they would fight, SEa, Air, and Land. The formation of these two teams was the catalyst for what would become the world's premiere naval special operations unit.

Shortly after their creation, the SEAL pups were deployed to the Caribbean in October 1962 during the Cuban Missile Crisis, and once again to the Dominican Republic in 1965. But the real watershed for the SEALs was in the civil war in Vietnam. The SEALs involvement in Vietnam began as an advisory mission in which SEAL advisors instructed the Vietnamese Navy in undertaking clandestine maritime operations. In February 1966, a detachment from SEAL Team 1 arrived in Vietnam to conduct direct-action missions. Operating out of Nha Be, in the Rung Sat Special Zone, this mission signaled the beginning of a SEAL presence that would eventually include eight SEAL platoons in-country on a continuing basis. A year later, members of SEAL Team 2 joined their fellow frogmen in the Southeast Asia conflict. Their mission included, but was not limited to, intelligence gathering, reconnaissance patrols, and direct-action missions (e.g., raids, prisoner snatches).

The following is an excerpt from U.S. Navy's doctrinal publication on naval warfare: "Strike the enemy at a time or place or in a manner for which he is unprepared. Catching the enemy off guard immediately puts him on the defensive, allowing us to drive events. The element of surprise is desirable, but it is not essential that the enemy be taken completely unaware—only that he becomes aware too late to react effectively. Concealing

During the Korean War, the Underwater Demolition Teams moved beyond the surf zone, tasked with conducting commando raids further in country. This evolution from water to land inspired future operations when the newly formed SEALs entered into the war in southeast Asia. The SEALs, who had no textbooks from which to work, still managed to develop new techniques to take the war to the enemy. The lessons learned from places in the delta, Rung Sat Special Zone, and a hundred other locations throughout the country are still valuable to current operators. National Archive

our capabilities and intentions by using covert techniques and deceptions gives us the opportunity to strike the enemy when he is not ready."

The term SEAL is an acronym for the methods of insertion and the environments in which they would fight—SEa, Air, and Land. The formation of the unit served as a catalyst for what would become the world's premiere naval special operations unit. The Vietnam War proved to be a watershed for the SEALs as they brought innovative tactics, techniques, and procedures to their new mission. Here a group of SEALs loads into a SEAL Team Assault Boat (STAB) as they prepare for an insertion. National Archives and Record Administration

The Vietnam War is regarded by many in the SEAL community as the crucible of today's Naval Special Warfare. In Vietnam, the SEALs took the war to the enemy, using guerilla methods and tactics, where and when he least expected it. They carried a wide assortment of weapons, including the Stoner machine gun shown here, which became a trademark with the SEALs. The SEALs became feared in the Mekong Delta, along the rivers, and in the jungles of Southeast Asia, earning the name "Men in the Green Faces." National Archives and Records Administration

During the war in Vietnam, the SEALs did exactly that; they took the war to the enemy, where and when he least expected it. These amphibious combatants were a quandary to the elusive Viet Cong. The SEALs did not build base camps upon the hilltops and call in artillery, so they were not Marines; neither did they enter the jungle en masse, making as much noise as a water buffalo sloshing through a rice paddy at noon, hence they could not be Army field units. When the SEALs went into the field they were not laden with ALICE packs and steel pots, nor did they go in with 30 or 40 men at a time.

The Navy SEALs had wide latitude in selection of weapons and equipment. The small teams could be attired in a variety of uniforms, from tiger stripes to blue jeans; some men wore coral shoes while others favored going in barefoot. Their weapons were also unique.

Naval Special Warfare-Medal of Honor Recipients

Three SEALs were awarded the Medal of Honor for action in Vietnam. They were Lieutenant Thomas R. Norris, Lieutenant Junior Grade Joseph Kerrey, and Petty Officer Michael Edwin Thornton.

Lieutenant Thomas R. Norris

Rank and organization: Lieutenant, U.S. Navy, SEAL Advisor, Strategic Technical Directorate Assistance Team; Headquarters: U.S. Military Assistance Command, Vietnam. Place and date: Quang Tri Province, Republic of Vietnam, April 10 to 13, 1972. Entered service at: Silver Spring, Maryland. Born: January 14, 1944, Jacksonville, Florida.

Citation: Lieutenant Norris completed an unprecedented ground rescue of two downed pilots deep within heavily controlled enemy territory in Quang Tri Province. On the night of April 10, Norris led a five-man patrol through 2,000 meters of heavily controlled enemy territory, located one of the downed pilots at daybreak, and returned to the Forward Operating Base (FOB). On April 11, after a devastating mortar and rocket attack on the small FOB, Norris led a three-man team on two unsuccessful rescue attempts for the second pilot. On the afternoon of the April 12, a forward air controller located the pilot and notified Norris. Dressed in fishermen disguises and using a sampan, Norris and one Vietnamese traveled throughout that night and found the injured pilot at dawn. Covering the pilot with bamboo and vegetation, they began the return journey and successfully evaded a North Vietnamese patrol. Approaching the FOB, they came under heavy machine-gun fire. Norris called in an air strike, which provided suppression fire and a smoke screen, to allow the rescue party to reach the FOB. With his outstanding display of decisive leadership, undaunted courage, and selfless dedication in the face of extreme danger, Norris enhanced the finest traditions of the U.S. Naval Service.

Lieutenant Junior Grade Joseph R. "Bob" Kerrey

Rank and organization: Lieutenant, Junior Grade, U.S. Naval Reserve, Sea, Air, and Land Team (SEAL). Place and date: Near Nha Trang Bay, Republic of Vietnam, March 14, 1969. Entered service at: Omaha, Nebraska. Born: August 27, 1943, Lincoln, Nebraska.

Citation: For conspicuous gallantry and intrepidity at the risk of his life above and beyond the call of duty while serving as a SEAL team leader during action against enemy aggressor (Viet Cong) forces. Acting in response to reliable intelligence, Lieutenant Kerrey led his SEAL team on a mission to capture important members of the enemy's area political cadre known to be located on an island in the bay of Nha Trang. In order to surprise the enemy, he and his team scaled a 350-foot sheer cliff to place themselves above the ledge on which the enemy was located. Splitting his team in two elements and coordinating both, Kerrey led his men in the treacherous downward descent to the enemy's camp. Just as they neared the end of their descent, intense enemy fire was directed at them, and Kerrey received massive injuries from a grenade that exploded at his feet and threw him backward onto the jagged rocks. Although bleeding profusely and suffering great pain, he displayed outstanding courage and presence of mind to immediately direct his element's fire into the heart of the enemy camp. Utilizing his radioman, Kerrey called in the second element's fire support, which caught the confused Viet Cong in a devastating crossfire. After successfully suppressing the enemy's fire, and although immobilized by his multiple wounds, he continued to maintain calm, superlative control as he ordered his team to secure and defend an extraction site. Lieutenant (J.G.) Kerrey resolutely directed his men, despite his near unconscious state, until he was eventually evacuated by helicopter. The havoc brought to the enemy by this very successful mission cannot be overestimated. The enemy soldiers who were captured provided critical intelligence to the allied effort. Kerrey's courageous and inspiring leadership, valiant fighting spirit, and tenacious devotion to duty in the face of almost overwhelming opposition sustain and enhance the finest traditions of the U.S. Naval Service.

Petty Officer Michael Edwin Thornton

Rank and organization: Petty Officer, U.S. Navy, Navy Advisory Group. Place and date: Republic of Vietnam, October 31, 1972. Entered service at: Spartanburg, South Carolina. Born: March 23, 1949, Greenville, South Carolina.

Citation: For conspicuous gallantry and intrepidity at the risk of his life above and beyond the call of duty while participating in a daring operation against enemy forces. Petty Officer Thornton, as Assistant U.S. Navy Advisor, along with a U.S. Navy lieutenant serving as Senior Advisor, accompanied a three-man Vietnamese Navy SEAL patrol on an intelligence-gathering and prisoner-capture operation against an enemy-occupied naval river base. Launched from a Vietnamese Navy junk in a rubber boat, the patrol reached land and was continuing on foot toward its objective, when it suddenly came under heavy fire from a numerically superior force. The patrol called in naval gunfire support and then engaged the enemy in a fierce firefight, accounting for many enemy casualties before moving back to the waterline to prevent encirclement. After learning that the Senior Advisor had been hit by enemy fire and was believed to be dead, Thornton returned through a hail of fire to the lieutenant's last position, quickly disposed of two enemy soldiers about to overrun the position, and succeeded in removing the seriously wounded and unconscious Senior Naval Advisor to the water's edge. He then inflated the lieutenant's lifejacket and towed him seaward for approximately two hours until they were picked up by support craft. By his extraordinary courage and perseverance, Thornton was directly responsible for saving the life of his superior officer and enabling the safe extraction of all patrol members, thereby upholding the highest traditions of the U.S. Naval Service.

In addition to the SEALs, a Medal of Honor was awarded to Petty Officer First Class James Williams. Although Williams was not a SEAL, he operated with the riverine forces, which would evolve into today's Special Boat Teams (SBTs).

Boatswain's Mate First Class (PO1) James E. Williams
Rank and organization: Boatswain's Mate First Class (PO1), U.S. Navy, River Section 531, My Tho, Vietnam. Place and date: Mekong River, October 31, 1966. Entered service at: Columbia, South Carolina. Born: November 13, 1930, Rock Hill, South Carolina.

Citation: For conspicuous gallantry and intrepidity at the risk of his life above and beyond the call of duty. Williams was serving as Boat Captain and Patrol Officer aboard River Patrol Boat 105 accompanied by another patrol boat when the patrol was suddenly taken under fire by two enemy sampans. Williams immediately ordered the fire returned, killing the crew of one enemy boat and causing the other sampan to take refuge in a nearby river inlet. Pursuing the fleeing sampan, the U.S. patrol encountered a heavy volume of small-arms fire from enemy forces at close range, occupying well-concealed positions along the riverbank. Maneuvering through this fire, the patrol confronted a numerically superior enemy force aboard two enemy junks and eight sampans augmented by heavy automatic weapons fire from ashore. In the savage battle that ensued, Williams, with utter disregard for his safety, exposed himself to the withering hail of enemy fire to direct counter-fire and inspire the actions of his patrol. Recognizing the overwhelming strength of the enemy force, Williams deployed his patrol to await the arrival of armed helicopters. In the course of his movement he discovered an even larger concentration of enemy boats. Not waiting for the arrival of the armed helicopters, he displayed great initiative and boldly led the patrol through the intense enemy fire and damaged or destroyed 50 enemy sampans and seven junks. After they had completed this phase of the action, and with the arrival of the armed helicopters, Williams directed the attack on the remaining enemy force. Now virtually dark, and although Williams was aware that his boats would become even better targets, he ordered the patrol boats' searchlights turned on to better illuminate the area and moved the patrol perilously close to shore to press the attack. Despite a waning supply of ammunition, the patrol successfully engaged the enemy ashore and completed the rout of the enemy force. Under the leadership of Williams, who demonstrated unusual professional skill and indomitable courage throughout the three-hour battle, the patrol accounted for the destruction or loss of 65 enemy boats and inflicted numerous casualties on the enemy personnel. His extraordinary heroism and exemplary fighting spirit, in the face of grave risks, inspired the efforts of his men to defeat a larger enemy force, and are in keeping with the finest traditions of the U.S. Naval Service.

While they did utilize the standard M16 service rifle, more often the patrols were armed with CAR15s, shotguns, and Stoner 63s. But the most important weapons the SEALs brought to bear were courage and tenacity, which those in the teams possessed in abundance. They fought the enemy on his own turf, using his guerilla methods and tactics. This earned SEALs the name "Men in the Green Faces." The SEALs became feared in the Mekong Delta, along the rivers, and throughout the forests of Southeast Asia. Regardless of the mission, the men of the Navy SEALs proved to be the quintessential waterborne commandos.

Supporting these warriors were the U.S. Navy riverine forces, the "brown water" Navy, and the slicks of the Sea Lords. Providing close air support were the Huey gunships of the Navy's Light Helicopter Attack Squadron 3 (HAL-3), the UH-IB Seawolves, and the O-10A Black Ponies. Throughout the scope of this work, their actions during the Vietnam War were heroic and distinguished in the chronicles of naval history and an integral part of Navy SEALs operations in Southeast Asia.

The lessons learned in Vietnam filled volumes for those who followed.

The last SEAL platoon departed Vietnam on December 7, 1971, and the last SEAL advisor left in March 1973. For actions in the Republic of Vietnam, Navy SEALs were awarded 3 Medals of Honor, 2 Navy Cross Medals, 42 Silver Star Medals, and 402 Bronze Star Medals.

In May 1983, all UDTs were redesignated as SEAL teams or swimmer delivery vehicle teams (SDVTs), and the underwater demolition teams were decommissioned. SDVTs have since been redesignated SEAL delivery vehicle teams.

Since Vietnam, SEALs have remained active with the operations in the Caribbean, Panama, and the Middle East.

OPERATION URGENT FURY

On October 25, 1983, Operation Urgent Fury began with the United States invasion of the Caribbean island of Grenada, which had been under expanding Cuban influence for some time. Following a failed military coup to overthrow the Communist leader, Maurice Bishop, President Ronald Reagan was concerned for the safety of the hundreds of Americans on the island. President Reagan determined an invasion was the solitary option to restore stability to the island nation.

The first of two SEAL missions on Grenada was the assault on the Governor-General Mansion in the St.

George area. The governor-general was never in dire danger, and the SEALs sustained only one operator wounded in an action that led to numerous People's Revolutionary Army (PRA) casualties. The second mission was a reconnaissance of the beach landing site and area adjacent to the Pearls Airport at the northern end of the island.

The Grenada operation was not without its cost to the special operations community. Four U.S. Navy SEALs were lost at sea during a "Rubber Duck" parachute insertion of the team. This tragedy hit the Special Operations forces (SOF) community especially hard.

Operation Urgent Fury was fraught with planning problems and the lack of standardization among the special operation units. These problems were factored into post-operation efforts to standardize many aspects of special operations doctrine and equipment across the armed services.

OPERATION JUST CAUSE

In December 1989, the United States initiated Operation Just Cause, the invasion of Panama. One of the primary missions was to hunt down and capture General Manuel Noriega, a rogue dictator and international drug trafficker. Answering concerns that Noriega might attempt to flee the country, SEALS were tasked with two missions to prevent his escape. These missions were carried out prior to the actual invasion at H-hour.

The first mission was to disable the general's boats, which were seen as a means of escape. Under the cover of darkness, SEALs infiltrated Balboa Harbor, where Noriega's power yachts were moored. Employing LAR-V closed-circuit rebreathers, the waterborne commandos approached the vessels. One team placed limpet mines on the stern of the first boat while the other team placed C4 plastic explosive around the twin propeller shafts of the other. The SEALs set the timers and exfiltrated the harbor, swimming to teammates waiting for them in combat rubber raiding craft (CRRCs). Twenty minutes later, a thunderous explosion ripped through the night; the two boats had been removed from any escape plan—mission accomplished.

Unfortunately, the other SEAL mission did not share the same success. The second mission assigned to the SEALs that night was the seizure of Paitilla Airfield and destruction of Noriega's Learjet in order to eliminate yet another escape route. Although the SEALs are highly trained and

During Operation Desert Storm, Navy SEALs performed numerous missions including direct action, special reconnaissance, and some that are still classified. Here, members of SEAL Team 5 practice ambush techniques in the Chocolate Mountains of California. Such tactics and procedures were used to carry out their mission in the Persian Gulf War.

skilled, Army Rangers typically take down airports, not Navy SEALs. Nevertheless, this was the mission the SEALs were tasked, and they would carry it out in the finest of SEAL tradition. SEALs normally work in small teams, usually an 8-man squad or 16-man platoon, but Paitilla raid called for 3 platoons—48 SEALs. The actual mission was accomplished, but at a very high cost; 6 of the SEALs were killed and 8 others were seriously wounded.

Following the Paitilla mission, new operational criteria were established for the employment of SOF units: Is this an appropriate SOF mission? Does it support the theater commander's campaign plan? Is it operationally feasible? Are the required resources available? Does the expected outcome justify the risk? Had these questions been asked and answered prior to the Paitilla raid, the SEALs would never have been committed.

OPERATION DESERT STORM

In Desert Storm a unit of six SEALs (five enlisted men led by Lieutenant Junior Grade Tom Dietz) successfully undertook Operation Deception, the object of which was to fake Iraqi troops into waiting for an amphibious invasion that would never come. They planted explosive charges a few hundred yards apart along a length of beach in Kuwait and Iraq and set the charges to detonate a few seconds apart. The mission was carried out about 25 miles from a base of the Iraqi elite Republican Guards. When the charges went off, large portions of two Iraqi

divisions were spotted by U.S. reconnaissance satellites as they moved toward the Gulf area and away from the main front of the Allied ground forces.

Two days after this mission, the SEALs received a message from the operation commander, General Norman Schwarzkopf, that read, "Enemy forces moving to beach. Allied forces going behind them. You have saved the lives of many of our fellow soldiers, sailors, airmen, and Marines. Bravo Zulu." This was high praise coming from "The Bear," who was not a strong proponent of special operations forces, an opinion that differed greatly after the war.

Following Desert Storm, Navy SEALs saw action in Somalia, Haiti, and Bosnia.

OPERATION ENDURING FREEDOM

Navy SEALs conducted special reconnaissance on suspected Al Qaeda and Taliban forces throughout Afghanistan, and SEAL teams performed a wide variety of missions, including sensitive-site exploitation (SSE) and search-and-destroy. The platoons found themselves in caves, houses, compounds, and underground complexes. Such responsibilities netted the SEALs tons of ammunition, weapons, and intelligence material on the terrorist forces.

A sensitive site is a geographically limited area with special diplomatic, informational, military, or economic

A member of Combined Joint Special Operation Task Force South, also referred to as Force Ka-Bar, conducts special reconnaissance (SR) on an undisclosed location in southern Afghanistan in support of Operation Enduring Freedom. In February 2002, TF Ka-Bar was credited with the capture of Mullah Kairullah Kahirkawa, a high-ranking Taliban leader. Official Task Force Ka-Bar

SEALs were inserted in the wasteland of Afghanistan to conduct special reconnaissance (SR) missions on suspected Al Qaeda and Taliban forces. They also undertook direct-action missions. Note that the SEAL on the left is carrying an antitank rocket launcher. U.S. Navy

U.S. Navy SEALs search for Al Qaeda and Taliban while conducting a sensitive-site exploitation (SSE) mission in the Jaji mountain region of eastern Afghanistan. Although the structure appears to be safe, the SEALs maintain security, as can be seen on the left foreground of the photo. Also worth noting is that on this mission, carried out in February 2002, the SEALs are wearing Gore-Tex gaiters to keep out the snow. U.S. Navy

Navy SEALs conducted special reconnaissance on suspected Al Qaeda and Taliban forces throughout the region. SEAL teams also performed sensitive-site exploitation (SSE) and search-and-destroy missions, among others. The platoons found themselves in caves, houses, compounds, and underground complexes. Such forays netted the SEALs tons of ammunition, weapons, and intelligence material on the terrorist forces, as seen here in this photo of a sensitive-site exploitation mission in Afghanistan. U.S. Navy

sensitivity to the United States. Examples of such sites would be suspected weapons or chemical factories, research facilities, or warehouses containing weapons of mass destruction, be they nuclear, biological, or chemical in nature. Other such sites are those at which a high-ranking enemy commander or regime leaders might be located.

A member of SEAL Team 3 observes the destruction of Al Qaeda munitions during a sensitive-site exploitation (SSE) mission in eastern Afghanistan during Operation Enduring Freedom. Note that this SEAL has made a modification to his battle-dress uniform with the addition of a cargo pocket to the shoulder of his three-color desert BDU. He is armed with an M4 with an Aimpoint optical sight. U.S. Navy

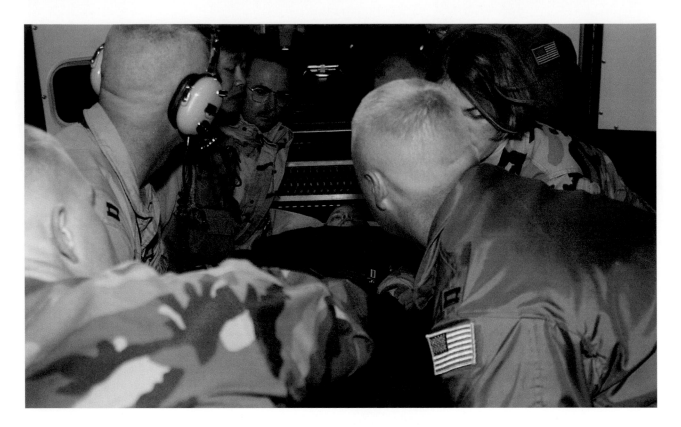

In the largest deployment of Naval Special Warfare operators since the Vietnam War, approximately 250 served in the area of Iraq. One of the highest profile special operations missions conducted during Operation Iraqi Freedom was the rescue of Private First Class Jessica Lynch by U.S. SOF units. SEALs played an integral part. In this photo, Jessica Lynch is being placed into an ambulance after arriving at Ramstein Air Base in Germany. U.S. Air Force

OPERATION IRAQI FREEDOM

In the largest NavSpecWar deployment since the Vietnam War, approximately 250 SEALs operated in and around Iraq. In addition to the SEALs, naval special warfare crewmen, naval intelligence, and communications specialists participated in Operation Iraqi Freedom, in-country and in Kuwait.

Navy SEALs were tasked with securing the hydro-electric Mukarayin Dam, its adjoining power station, and facilities. Inserted under the cover of darkness from AFSOC Pave Low helicopters, a SEAL and Polish Grom joint-commando team assaulted the dam, which is approximately 60 miles northeast of Baghdad.

In another operation, Navy SEALs using high-speed Mark V special warfare craft of the U.S. Navy Special Boat Units assaulted two Iraqi offshore oil platforms, Mina al Bakar and Khawr al Amaya, in the Persian Gulf. Snipers in orbiting helicopters provided cover fire as the waterborne commandos assaulted the platforms. The seizure of these oil platforms assured that Hussein forces could not repeat the ecological assault they had carried

out during the first Gulf War, when they dumped vast quantities of raw, crude oil into the Persian Gulf.

The SEALs were also instrumental in clearing mines from the waterways to be used by naval and humanitarian vessels, as well as other missions.

One of the best-known special operations missions conducted during Operation Iraqi Freedom was the rescue of Private First Class Jessica Lynch by American Special Operation force units. SEALs played an integral part in the rescue. On the night of April 1, Marines opened an assault in An Nasiriya as a diversion meant to draw attention away form the hospital. According to CENTCOM reports, the operation consisted of Army Rangers, Air Force pilots and combat controllers, U.S. Marines, and Navy SEALs. It was a classic joint operation undertaken by some of our nation's finest warriors, who are dedicated to the credo, "Never leave a comrade behind." The rescue also exemplifies the successful culmination, so far, of the joint planning and operations doctrines that emerged from the 1983 Grenada operation.

areas of operational responsibility (AORs) throughout the world. The inception of NSW 21 has put into practice substantial changes in how the SEALs train, organize, and deploy. The implementation of these changes will provide NavSpecWarCom with a more efficient use of its forces around the world as the United States continues its fight in the Global War on Terrorism (GWT).

NAVAL SPECIAL ORGANIZATION

An integral part of NSW 21 was the reorganization of the NSW squadrons. The new NSW squadron brings together under one command the SEAL teams, SEAL delivery vehicles teams (SDVTs), and special boat units, which are now called special boat teams (SBTs). Attached to these squadrons are a mobile communications detachment, a tactical cryptology team, and experts in explosive ordnance disposal (EOD).

The new squadron now goes through a two-year cycle encompassing four six-month phases—individual-level training, unit training, pre-deployment squadron train, and an operational deployment of all hands. In addition to the operators and support units, the SEAL team commander, executive officer, and command master chief deploy with the men, a contrast to the previous practice in which they remained stateside.

SEAL TEAMS

SEAL teams are the Navy's waterborne commandos, multi-functional combat forces trained, organized, and equipped to plan, carry out, and support special missions in a variety of operational environments. SEAL teams perform direct action (DA), unconventional warfare (UW), foreign internal defense (FID), special reconnaissance (SR), and counterterrorist (CT) operations primarily in maritime and riverine environments, referred to as "blue water" and "brown water," respectively.

In 2002, two additional teams—SEAL Team 7 and SEAL Team 10—were created, thus bringing the total number of SEAL teams to eight. Teams 1, 3, 5, and 7 are located on the West Coast, at Naval Amphibious Base, Coronado, California; Teams 2, 4, 8, and 10 operate from Naval Amphibious Base, Little Creek, Virginia, on the East Coast. Operations include sabotage, demolition, intelligence collection, hydrographic reconnaissance, and training and advising friendly military forces in the conduct of naval and joint special operations. The expansion of the teams from six to eight was accomplished without increasing the actual number of SEAL operators, but by reducing the platoon complement from eight down to six per team.

Officer-in-Charge (OIC), Alpha Platoon, SEAL Team 5. A SEAL platoon normally is comprised of 16 members, broken down into two 8-man squads. The lieutenant is responsible for the overall conduct of the mission from the time the team boards the helicopter or other insertion vessel, to the action at target, to the time it takes to exfil the platoon safely from the area. Along with the point man, he is the primary navigator. A SEAL platoon is one of the most lethal weapons an enemy may ever encounter. This Officer-in-Charge is camouflaged and ready to fade away into the desert brush.

NAVAL SPECIAL WARFARE 21

In 2002, the commander of all naval special warfare and the highest ranking SEAL, Rear Admiral Eric T. Olson, directed the SEALS to restructure the way in which the team were organized and deployed, an undertaking referred to as Naval Special Warfare 21 (NSW 21). Prior to this reorganization, SEAL teams were assigned to various

Training

GENERAL REQUIREMENTS

The SEAL program is open only to men. All SEAL candidates must meet the following requirements: eyesight 20/20 or correctable to 20/20, with no color blindness; 28 years old or less; must be a U.S. citizen and obtain security clearance; and must pass a diving physical.

BASIC UNDERWATER DEMOLITION/SEALS (BUD/S)

INDOCTRINATION

BUD/S indoctrination, five weeks in duration, is the bonding factor between all who wear the SEAL trident. Officers and enlisted go through identical, demanding training cycles. As a result, when an officer is assigned to command a SEAL platoon, he is commanding because he has earned this right. It is not because he is filling a slot in a rotational assignment. This is a mandatory course designed to give the student an understanding of the techniques and performance required of him.

The first obstacle a student faces is the BUD/S Physical Screen Test, which he must pass in order to class up and begin training. At the end of the indoctrination course, he will be given a more advanced version of the BUD/S Physical Screen Test, which must be passed in order to enter the First Phase of BUD/S.

FIRST PHASE—BASIC CONDITIONING

First Phase is eight weeks in length. During this time continued physical conditioning in the areas of running, swimming, and calisthenics is emphasized and grows increasingly difficult as the weeks progress. Students participate in weekly four-mile runs in boots and must undertake timed obstacle courses. They swim ocean distances up to two miles in fins and learn small-boat seamanship.

The first two weeks of First Phase are preparation for the third week, known as "Hell Week." Students participate in five and a half days of continuous training, with a maximum of four hours of sleep for the entire week. This week is designed as the ultimate test of one's physical and mental motivation while in First Phase. During Hell Week, the students learn the value of the SEAL Teams' mantra: TEAMWORK! The remaining five weeks are devoted to teaching methods for conducting hydrographic surveys, preparing hydrographic charts, and instruction in basic maritime operations.

DROWNPROOFING

SEALs are at home in the water. To achieve the required level of comfort, they go through drownproofing. The purpose of this training is to infuse confidence in the water and aptitude even in the most intense situations.

A student has his hands tied behind his back and his feet bound; he then enters the water in the 9-foot-deep combat training tank and must bob for 5 minutes. After this time he is instructed to remain on the surface and float for 5 minutes. After floating, he swims 100 meters, then bobs again for 2 minutes, demonstrating underwater forward and reverse flips. The trainee successfully completes the evolution when he goes to the bottom of the tank, retrieves his mask with his teeth, and completes 5 bobs.

Successful completion of the drownproofing evolution demonstrates to the training cadre and trainee both comfort and competency in the water. This drill is a principal indication of a student's ability to successfully complete the maritime aspect of BUD/S training.

SECOND PHASE—DIVING

By completing First Phase, the prospective SEAL must prove to the instructor staff that he is motivated to participate in more in-depth training. The diving phase is eight weeks in length. Physical training continues during this period, and the times are lowered for the four-mile run, two-mile swim, and obstacle course.

Second Phase concentrates on combat SCUBA (self-contained underwater breathing apparatus). Students are taught two types of SCUBA: open circuit (compressed air) and closed circuit (100 percent oxygen). They participate in a progressive dive schedule that emphasizes the basic-combat swimmer skills necessary to qualify as a combat diver. These skills enable a swimmer to operate tactically and to complete his combat objective.

BUD/S—Basic Underwater Demolition/SEAL—training motto: "The Only Easy Day Was Yesterday!" This is the thread that binds all SEALs. During this intense physical training, the phrases, "It pays to be a winner," and "There is no 'I' in TEAM" become ingrained into the SEAL's persona and are taken up as the mantra for the students moving from evolution to evolution. Here, students from Class 244 conduct surf-passage drills. It is here, in BUD/S, where a man learns what he is made of, for there are no timeouts on the battlefield.

THIRD PHASE–LAND WARFARE

The demolitions, reconnaissance, weapons, and tactics phase is nine weeks long. Physical training intensifies and grows more strenuous as the run distances increase and minimum passing times are lowered for the runs, swims, and obstacle course. Third Phase concentrates on teaching land navigation, small-unit tactics, patrolling, rappelling, military land and underwater explosives, and weapons.

The final four weeks of Third Phase are spent on the Maritime Operations Facility on San Clemente Island, where students apply in a practical environment the techniques acquired throughout training.

POST-BUD/S SCHOOLS

BUD/S graduates receive three weeks of basic parachute training at Army Airborne School in Fort Benning, Georgia, prior to returning to the Naval Special Warfare Center for fifteen weeks of SEAL Qualification Training (SQT). Upon successful completion of SQT, qualified personnel are awarded a Naval Special Warfare Trident insignia. Each is then assigned to a SEAL Team.

Training does not stop here because a wide range of advanced schools are available. Advanced courses include sniper school, dive supervisor school, language training, SEAL tactical communication, and many others.

Water covers 71 percent of the surface. Of the world's populace, 60 percent is located within 60 miles of a shoreline, which provides access to 148 countries via the water. All but 43 countries have coastal access. Naval Special Warfare Command's implementation of NSW 21 provides for an efficient use of its forces around the world as the United States continues its fight against global terrorism.

SEAL PLATOONS

The SEAL platoon is the largest operational component that will generally be employed to conduct a tactical mission. A platoon consists of 16 SEALs who may be divided into two squads or four elements. A typical SEAL platoon is commanded by a Navy lieutenant (O-3) who is the officer-in-charge (OIC); an assistant officer-in-charge (AOIC); and third officer, usually a recent graduate of the

program, who may be assigned to prepare him for his next platoon, in which he will assume the role of AOIC. All SEAL platoon personnel are dive, parachute, and demolitions qualified.

The Special Operations Command lists the capabilities of SEAL teams to include: "Destroy or sabotage enemy shipping, port and harbor facilities, bridges, railway lines, communications centers, and other lines of communications (LOC) in and around maritime areas and riverine environments to undermine the morale or degrade the military, political, or economic strength of the enemy. Infiltration and exfiltration of SEALs may be by submarine, surface vessel, aircraft, or land vehicle. SEAL teams conduct reconnaissance, surveillance, and other intelligence-gathering tasks, including capture of key personnel. On a limited scale, they are involved in civic action tasks that are normally associated with foreign internal defense and humanitarian actions (HA) operations (i.e., medical aid, elementary civil engineering activities, and boat operations and maintenance for the indigenous population). Organize, train, assist, and advise U.S., allied, and other friendly military or paramilitary forces in the conduct of any of the above tasks. Integrate NSW task organizations into fleet task forces or groups to plan, coordinate, and conduct maritime special operations. SEALs operate in desert, arctic, jungle, urban, riverine, or maritime environments. SEAL teams may be employed in direct support of conventional naval and maritime operations."

SPECIAL MISSION UNITS

The U.S. Department of Defense has acknowledged the formation and maintenance of selected special mission units (SMUs). These SMUs are specifically organized, trained, and equipped to conduct an assortment of highly classified special operations missions. A primary mission is the deployment of covert action teams to combat terrorism and counter terrorist use of weapons of mass destruction (WMD). These SMUs are usually under the direct supervision of the highest command levels, typically the National Command Authority (NCA). They are specially manned, equipped, and trained to deal with an assortment of international threats. The SMUs are under the control of the Joint Special Operations Command (JSOC), which is understood to include the Army's Combat Applications Group (CAG) and the Naval Special Warfare Development Group (DEVGRU).

An example of an SMUs is Task Force 11. The mission of Task Force 11 is to hunt down and capture and/or kill high-ranking Taliban and Al Qaeda terrorists, wherever they may be. Based out of the JSOC, in a secure compound at Pope Air Force Base, North Carolina (next to Fort Bragg, home of the Army's Special Operations Command), members of the highly covert counterterrorism (CT) group of U.S. Navy SEALS from the Naval Special Warfare Development Group are tasked, along with the Army Delta Force, with conducting counterterrorist operations including but not limited to direct-action strikes, intelligence-gathering, and special reconnaissance in denied enemy areas. The SMUs in Afghanistan work in close proximity to track down enemy movements, locate positions, monitor communications, and, when the opportunity presents itself, kill the terrorists.

Regarding the mission of Task Force 11, White House Press Secretary Ari Fleischer stated, "There remains danger in Afghanistan. And as the President said at the very beginning of this battle last October [2001], this will be a war that's going to go in various phases, some of which will be visible; some will not." Another American official commented on the mission of the SMU, "They are the best. They are going after high-value targets."

Another example of an SMU is Task Force 20. Similar to that of Task Force 11, the mission of Task Force 20 was to locate and capture or kill high-ranking members of the former Iraqi regime, including Saddam Hussein and his sons. As with other such SMUs, Task Force 20 includes Army and Navy CT operators.

NAVAL SPECIAL WARFARE DEVELOPMENT GROUP (NSWDG)

The NSWDG, more commonly referred to as DEVGRU and called DevGroup, is the maritime version of the Army combat applications group (CAG), better known as Delta Force. DEVGRU was created the mid-1990s following the declared disbanding of SEAL Team 6. The Navy's official comments on the unit state its mission is to create, test, and evaluate new tactics, weapons, and equipment for the NSW community. DEVGRU, which is based in Dam Neck, Virginia, is believed to stand at a strength of approximately 400 operators and support personnel who are divided into four combat teams and one training team. DEVGRU is responsible for U.S. counterterrorist operations in the maritime environment. Sources have indicated the unit is in every respect a continuation of Seal Team 6.

Members of DEVGRU are constantly training throughout the United States and in conjunction with our allies throughout the world. Through the use of exchange programs and joint trainings exercises and missions, these highly skilled CT operators may find themselves in

The SEAL Trident badge, known among the teams as the "Budweiser." It is the largest insignia in the U.S. military and is worn by less than one percent of U.S. Navy personnel. These are the warriors of the Navy SEALs, who often get the missions no one else wants and, if you listen to the operators in the teams, the missions "no one else can do."

the company of British Special Boat Squadron (SBS) units, and British or Australian Special Air Service (SAS) teams as well as other highly covert special operations operators from other allied forces. The intense training is characterized by the maxim, "The more you sweat in peace, the less you'll bleed in war."

SEA-WATERCRAFT

Members of SBT22 move through the waterways to extract a patrol during a training exercise.

SPECIAL BOAT TEAMS (SBTs)

Special boat teams are organized, trained, and equipped to operate a variety of special-operations surface craft in both the maritime and riverine environments. Their unique capabilities in the littoral battle space includes the capability to transition from the blue-water open ocean to beach landing sites to operations within inland maritime lines of communication (i.e., the riverine environment referred to as brown water).

The mission of an SBT is to employ, operate, and maintain a variety of surface combatant craft to conduct and support naval and joint special operations, riverine warfare, and coastal patrol and interdiction. These craft range from the large patrol coastal (PC) craft to air-deployable rigid-hull inflatable boats (RIBs). The SBT is capable of infiltrating and exfiltrating forces, providing small-caliber gunfire support, conducting coastal patrol, surveillance, harassment, and interdiction of maritime lines of communication, FID operations, deception operations, combat search-and-rescue (CSAR) operations, and armed escort.

Qualified members of Naval Special Warfare's Special Boat Teams (NSW SBTs) are authorized to wear this new warfare pin, designated specifically for SWCC.

PATROL COASTAL CLASS SHIP

The patrol coastal ship has a primary mission of coastal patrol and interdiction, and a secondary mission of supporting naval special warfare. Primary employment missions include forward presence, monitoring and detection operations, escort operations, non-combatant evacuation, and foreign internal defense. The PC class operates in low-intensity environments. NSW operational missions include long-range SEAL insertion/extraction, tactical swimmer operations, intelligence collection, operational deception, and coastal/riverine support. PCs normally operate in two-boat detachments to enhance support and facilitate their assignment of one mobile support team (MST).

Special Boat Teams in History

The Special Boat Teams can trace their origins to the "Brown Water" Navy in service during the Vietnam War. These riverine forces were instrumental in bringing the war to the elusive Viet Cong and North Vietnamese Army. Starting from scratch in 1965, by the end of their involvement in the conflict the force had expanded into three task forces totaling more than 700 craft and more than 35,000 men. The development of a dynamic riverine warfare capability during the Vietnam War was the forerunner of the modern Special Warfare Combatant–craft Crewman (SWCC). SEAL operations were supported by Mobile Support Teams, which supplied combat-craft support for their operations (i.e., patrol boat riverine (PBR) and swift boat sailors).

Boat Support Unit 1 was established in February 1964 under Naval Operations Support Group, Pacific, to operate the newly reinstated patrol torpedo, fast (PTF) program. This newly organized unit operated high-speed craft in support of Naval Special Warfare forces with as much flare as the legendary PT-boat crews of World War II.

In 1965, Boat Support Squadron 1 began training patrol craft, fast (PCF), or swift, boat crews for Vietnamese coastal patrol and interdiction operations. As the Vietnam mission expanded into the riverine environment, additional craft, tactics, and training evolved for riverine patrol and SEAL support.

In January 1967, the Naval Inshore Operations Training Center was commissioned in Mare Island, California, to provide instruction and practical training for the potential crewmen of Task Force 116 (River Patrol) and Task Force 117 (River Assault).

Training for the crews of Task Force 115 (Coastal Surveillance) was conducted at the Naval Amphibious Base in Coronado, California. During this eleven-week River Assault Craft training program, sailors were given an overview to the special characteristics of joint operations, counterinsurgency, SERE (survival, evasion, resistance, and escape), and every element of riverine warfare.

SWCC is the acronym for Special Warfare Combatant-craft Crewmen. The members of SWCC pilot an assortment of special warfare craft from RIBs to PCs. They support SEALs and other Special Operations Command forces in their maritime and riverine missions, and conduct unconventional small-boat operations, such as coastal/riverine patrols.

Today the SWCC of the Special Boat Teams perform their missions with the same precision, tenacity, and lethality as their SEAL comrades. SWCC units utilize a combination of specialized training, equipment, and tactics in completion of special operation missions worldwide. Although they will be the first to tell you they are not SEALs, their contribution to Naval Special Warfare is an integral part of the community. You cannot tell the story of the SEALs without including the men of the SBTs. SWCC units are minutely trained in all environments, and they are the masters of maritime Special Operations.

The PC is armed with a variety of weapon systems for offensive and defensive operations. The machine gun system (MGS) MK38 is a 25mm automatic gun system that provides ships with defensive and offensive gunfire capability for the engagement of a variety of surface targets. It is designed to provide close-range defense against patrol boats; swimmers; floating mines; and various targets ashore, including enemy personnel, lightly armored vehicles, and terrorist threats. One crewman is required for operation, and there are two for maintenance. Due to the maximum elevation rate of 55 degrees, the MK38 has only limited antiair warfare importance. For this reason, the MK38 is primarily used against surface targets such as mines and boats.

The M242 auto-cannon is an externally powered, dual-feed, single-barrel weapon that may be fired in semiautomatic or automatic modes. In the automatic mode, the rate of fire is approximately 175 rounds per minute. The

The flagship of the Special Boat Teams is the patrol coastal (PC) craft. With a length of 170 feet, a beam of 25 feet, a draft of 7.8 feet, and displacement of 328.5 tons, it is the largest craft in the SBT inventory. The fast, agile PC is powered by four Paxman diesels and two Caterpillar generators that provide the craft with a speed of 30-plus knots and a range of 3,000 nautical miles. Not only is the PC fast, it is a formidable weapons platform that provides the SEALs with fire support during their missions. The PC is armed with a MK38 25mm rapid-fire gun, a MK96 25mm rapid-fire gun, Stinger missiles, four pintles that can support any combination of M2 .50-caliber heavy machine guns, M60 machine guns, MK19 grenade launchers, small arms, or a MK52 Mod 0 chaff decoy launching system. The PC has a complement of 4 officers and 24 enlisted, as well as berthing space for a SEAL squad or other SOF detachment.

The MK96 MOD 0 stabilized 25mm gun mount in use on the PC-1 *Cyclone*-class patrol coastal ships. The 25mm ammunition is the same as that used on the Marine light-armored vehicles (LAVs) and the Army's Bradley infantry flighty vehicle.

Also known as "Bushmaster," this weapon is a naval-ized version of the "chain gun," an externally powered weapon developed by Hughes for the U.S. Army as the MK242. The MK38 replaced the obsolete MK67 20mm guns, which had high-maintenance requirements. The Army's MK242 gun entered service in the 1970s, and the Navy's MK38 followed in 1988. Since then, the MK38 has been employed aboard various combatant and auxiliary ships in Middle East Force escort operations and during Operations Desert Shield and Desert Storm.

There are five .50-caliber heavy machine guns on a PC, including these dual-mounted .50s. The M2 is 61.42 inches in length and weighs in at 84 pounds. A PC crewman scans the horizon for contacts aboard the *Cyclone*-class patrol boat USS *Chinook* (PC-9) during Operation Iraqi Freedom. U.S. Navy

M242 does not depend on gases for operation; it utilizes an electric motor located in the receiver. Ammunition feeding, loading, firing, extraction, and ejection are all performed by the internal motor. The MK88 machine-gun mount is trained and elevated by the weapon's gunner. In the event of a major malfunction, the M242 auto-cannon can be removed from the mount and another auto-cannon installed by two people in five minutes.

A Mark V of Special Boat Team, which provides platforms for the insertion of SEALs. The Mark V can be used to insert or extract any U.S. Special Operations forces (SOF) team. With a speed in excess of 45 knots and an assorted weapons array, the boat crews can lay down suppressive fire in support of extracting operators from a "hot" pickup zone.

MARK V SPECIAL OPERATIONS CRAFT (SOC)

The Mark V special operations craft is a versatile, high-performance combatant craft introduced into the NSW Special Boat Squadron (SBR) inventory to improve maritime special operations capabilities.

The primary mission of the MK V SOC is as a medium-range insertion and extraction platform for SEALs and

The aft deck of a Mark V shows the four weapons stations built into this special-ops watercraft. On the starboard side are two .50-caliber heavy machine guns, and on the port side are two MK19 40mm machine grenade launchers. A combat rubber raiding craft (CRRC), or Zodiac, sits poised on the rear deck, which is slanted to facilitate launch and recovery of the CRRC during infiltration and extraction operations.

A coxswain at the controls of a Mark V.

Seen here is the Special Mission Seat manufactured by STIDD. This operator seat/bolster features contoured headrest, reclining backrest, 4-point harness, and locking armrests. To function in the saltwater environment, the seat is constructed of fully corrosion-resistant aluminum.

other special-operations forces in low- to medium-threat environments. The secondary mission is limited coastal patrol and interdiction, specifically limited-duration patrol, and low- to medium-threat coastal interdiction. The MK V SOC will normally operate in a two-craft detachment with a mobile support team.

The mobile support team (MST) provides technical assistance and maintenance support during mission turnaround. The MK V SOC is fundamentally a single-sortie system with a 24-hour turnaround time. The typical MK V SOC mission duration is 12 hours. The MK V is fully interoperable with the PC ships and NSW RIBs. As such, all could be employed from a forward operating base (FOB) in a cooperative effort. A MK V SOC detachment, consisting of two craft and support equipment, is deployable on two USAF C-5 aircraft into the theater within 48 hours of notification. A detachment is transportable over land on existing roadways. Detachments are not configured or manned to provide their own security, messing, or berthing for personnel while forward-deployed.

The Browning M2 .50-caliber heavy machine gun has been in service since World War II. It is an automatic, belt-fed, recoil-operated, air-cooled machine gun. Ammunition may be fed from either side via a disintegrating metallic link-belt. Capable of single-shot and full-automatic fire, this gun can be mounted on ground mounts and most vehicles as an antipersonnel and antiaircraft weapon. The M2 typically provides suppressive fire for offensive and defensive purposes. This weapon can be used effectively against personnel; light armored vehicles; low- and slow-flying aircraft; and small boats. The machine gun shown here is mounted on the stern of a SOCR on patrol in the waterways of southern Iraq during Operation Iraqi Freedom.

The MK19 40mm grenade machine gun has a firing rate of more than 350 grenades per minute at an effective range exceeding 2,200 meters. Manufactured by Saco Defense Industries, it has a length of 43.1 inches and weighs in at 137 pounds, of which 72.5 pounds is the weapon alone.

The MK19 is an air-cooled, blow-back operated, fully automatic weapon. It fires an assortment of 40mm grenades from a disintegrating metallic link-belt feed. These rounds include the M430 HEDP 40mm grenade, which will penetrate armor up to 2 inches thick and will produce fragments that can kill personnel within 5 meters and wound personnel within 15 meters of the point of impact.

RIGID-HULL INFLATABLE BOAT (RIB)

The 30-foot rigid-hull inflatable boat is a high-speed, high-buoyancy, and extreme-weather craft with the primary mission of insertion/extraction of SEAL tactical elements from enemy-occupied beaches. The RIB is constructed of glass-reinforced plastic with an inflatable-tube gunwale made of a new hypalon (neoprene/nylon) reinforced fabric. The RIB has demonstrated the ability to operate in light-load condition in sea state six and winds of 45 knots. For other than heavy-weather coxswain training, operations are limited to sea state five and winds of 34 knots or less. A 30-foot NSW RIB carries a crew of three with room for a full SEAL squad.

SWCC crews operating a RIB during Operation Iraqi Freedom. The RIBs were utilized for ship-to-shore insertion and extraction of SEAL platoons. U.S. Navy

The Rigid Inflatable Boat (RIB) is a high-speed, high-buoyancy, extreme-weather craft with the primary mission of insertion/extraction of SpecOps and SEAL teams from enemy beaches. The RIB hull is made of glass-reinforced plastic.

SPECIAL OPERATIONS CRAFT, RIVERINE (SOCR)

The special operations craft, riverine, is the U.S. Navy's latest watercraft fielded by the SBTs. The SOCR is designed as a fast boat with an ample cargo and weapons capacity, and the capability to operate effectively along inland waterways. The SOCR replaces the coastal assault craft (CAC) and the aging patrol boat, light (PBL) formally

Here, SEALs and SWCC train with Philippine Armed Forces aboard a RIB during joint training in support of Operation Enduring Freedom. The RIBs are 36 feet long with a draft of 2 feet, 11 inches. The craft is powered by 470-horsepower twin Caterpillar 3126 Diesel engines that project water through KaMeWa FF280 water jets to achieve a top speed of 45 knots and a range of more than 200 nautical miles. U.S. Navy

The SOCR is 33 feet long, 5 feet longer then its predecessor, the CAC. It has a 9-foot beam, drafts 2 feet, and draws only 8 inches of water at speed. The aluminum hull makes the craft light enough to be air transportable by U.S. Air Force cargo aircraft and rotary aircraft currently in the SOF inventory, i.e., MH47 Chinook and MH53 Pave Low helicopters. SOCOM

Seen here is the SOCR's coxswain station, which is encapsulated by armor plate, or "chicken plate," as it is referred to by the crews. This plate provides protection to the coxswain as well as the instrumentation and communications equipment.

Located just aft of the coxswain position is more navigation and communication equipment, as well as a remote fire-control station. The SWCC personnel are afforded some protection and concealment as they engage an assortment of weapons systems.

used in riverine operations. The SOCR is 33-feet long with a 9-foot beam; it drafts only 2 feet of water and draws only 8 inches of water at speed. It is powered by twin 440-horsepower Yanmar diesel engines, which provide rapid acceleration up to a rated top speed of 42 knots.

The craft provides SOCOM with a potent riverine force in position faster, with more capacity, and requiring less maintenance. The hull is fabricated from aluminum, which makes it light, strong, and capable of carrying up to 20,500 pounds in personnel and combat gear. It also means the craft is very transportable. If the SBTs need to get the craft onsite in a hurry, the SOCR can be transported by U.S. Air Force cargo aircraft and medium-lift helicopters such as the MH-47 Chinook and MH-53 Pave Low SOF helicopters.

A view of the SOCR from the bow toward the stern of the craft.

A view of the SOCR from the stern to the bow, over the engine compartment.

M240 machine gun mounted on a riverine craft of SBT22. This medium machine gun is the replacement for the older M60 series. Manufactured by Fabrique Nationale, it has a length of 47.5 inches and weighs 24.2 pounds. It takes the same 7.62mm round as the M60, with an effective range of 1.1 miles. The M240 has three cyclic settings: 650, 750, and 950 rounds per minute. In addition to the improved accuracy of the weapon, it should be noted that the maintenance is improved over the M60 because no part of the system can be put in backward.

The hull of the Special Operations Craft, Riverine, incorporates ballistic armor for protection, and the gunwale has five mounts to support a variety of weapons. The systems that can be mounted include the M240 7.62mm medium machine gun, the M2 .50-caliber heavy machine gun, the MK19 40mm grenade machine gun; and the GAU-17/A 7.62mm minigun. These weapons, along with those of the crew and the SEALs on board, make the SOCR a force to be reckoned with.

The stern view of the "Jenny 1," SOCR number 14 of Special Boat Team 22. This provides a clear view of the single Hamilton H3292 water jet, which gives the SOCR its great mobility and agile maneuverability.

"Ma Deuce" .50-caliber machine gun mounted on a CAC. This weapon has an effective range of 2,000 meters and a maximum effective range of 1,830 meters, with a cyclic rate of fire of 550 rounds per minute. Here, a U.S. Navy Special Warfare Combatant Craft crewman sits beside his .50-caliber machine gun mounted on the stern of a SOCR as it transits the southern waterways of Iraq during Operation Iraqi Freedom. U.S. Navy

The GAU-17/A 7.62mm "minigun" is used to provide a lightweight high-rate-of-fire support weapon for SEAL operations. The minigun is a six-barrel, electrically driven, rotary-action, percussion-fired weapon that can be set for 3,000 or 6,000 rounds per minute. When mounted on the SOCR, it is supplied by a 1,500- or 4,500-round ammunition container to deliver the linked 7.62 rounds on demand. The GAU-17/A weapon system consists of a gun-control assembly with electrical cables, gun drive motor, a MAU-201/A or a MAU-56 delinking feeder, flexible ammunition feed chutes, and an ammunition storage system.

COMBAT RUBBER RAIDING CRAFT (CRRC)

The combat rubber raiding craft (CRRC) is a Zodiac F470 inflatable boat used for clandestine surface insertion and extraction of SEAL teams. The CRRC can be employed to land and recover SEALs from over the horizon. It has a low visual electronic signature and is capable of being cached by its crew once ashore.

When using a 35- to 55-horsepower outboard motor, the Zodiac is fast and quiet. Each fuel bladder allows the craft approximately one hour of operation with an average load of six men and their equipment. The low profile and fabric provide little or no radar signature to be detected by hostile forces. The CRRC is extremely versatile; it can be deck-launched or locked-out from submarines and other boats. It can be air dropped via parachute or other deployable methods from an assortment of fixed- and rotary-wing aircraft.

SEAL delivery vehicle teams entered the submersible field in the 1960s, but their ancestry may be intertwined with the Italian and British combat swimmers and wet submersibles of World War II. In 1960, the Coastal Systems Center developed the MK 7 SEAL delivery vehicle, the first to be used in the Navy. This wet SDV was a free-flooding submersible of the type in use today. With further development, the MK 8 and MK 9 followed in the late 1970s. Today's MK 8 Mod 1 wet submersible and the advanced SEAL delivery system (ASDS)—a dry submersible—provide NSW with an unprecedented capability that combines the attributes of clandestine underwater mobility and the combat swimmer's own covert capabilities.

There are two SDV teams operating under the Naval Special Warfare Command. The first, SDVT-1, is located on Ford Island at Naval Station, Pearl Harbor, Hawaii, and the second, SDVT-2, is at Naval Amphibious Base, Little Creek, Virginia. These teams are specifically trained to use the MK 8 SDV as an insertion and extraction platform. Members of the SDV teams have graduated from the SDV School, which is a ten-week course for SEALs who have earned their coveted SEAL Trident pin. Training at the SDV School teaches the SEALs everything they will need to know regarding the operation of the MK 8. It is worth noting that, unlike the SWCC, the SDV team members are SEALs and, as such, are fully trained and capable of conducting any SEAL mission. They just happen to focus on this specialized insertion platform.

A CRRC is prepared for deployment off the fantail of the nuclear-powered submarine USS *Kamehameha* (SSN-642) off the coast of Oahu, Hawaii. Defense Visual Image Center

The Zodiac F-470 Combat Rubber Raiding Craft (CRRC) is one of the primary methods used for inserting SEALs. It is 15 feet, 5 inches in length with a beam of 6 feet, 3 inches. It has a draft of 2 feet and weighs 265 pounds without the motor and fuel. With motor mounted, it has a speed of 18 knots and its range is dependent on how much fuel is carried aboard. It will carry eight SEALs.

SEAL DELIVERY VEHICLE (SDV) TASK UNITS

SEAL delivery vehicle (SDV) task units units are organized, trained, and equipped to operate and maintain combat submersible systems, and conduct specialized missions utilizing the host submarine's dry deck shelter (DDS) as an insertion/extraction platform. SDV unit capabilities include limited direct-action (DA) missions, such as port and harbor antishipping attacks and raids. Special mission units, using the SDV from the DDS, or the DDS alone, can conduct a variety of DA missions in the maritime environment. SDV task units conduct hydrographic reconnaissance and other intelligence-gathering missions as well as infiltrate, exfiltrate, and resupply SEAL teams.

The SDV task unit is a temporary operational element employed to plan, coordinate, and command submersible systems operations from specially configured submarines equipped with dry deck shelters. The SEAL Delivery Vehicle task unit is normally commanded by an SDV team commanding officer or executive officer, and it is composed of one or more SDV or SEAL platoons. While deployed on board a submarine with a DDS attached, the DDS platoon commander reports to the submarine commanding officer as a department head and does not fall under the operational control of the SDV task unit commander.

DRY DECK SHELTER (DDS)

The dry deck shelter allows for the launch and recovery of a SEAL delivery vehicle or combat rubber raiding craft (CRRC) with personnel from a submerged submarine. It consists of three interconnected modules constructed as one integral unit. Each of the components is capable of independent pressurization to a minimum depth of 130 feet. The first module is a hangar in which an SDV or CRRC is stowed. This section is large enough to house either an SDV, or a platoon of SEALs with CRRCs. The second module is a transfer trunk to allow the SEALs to enter between the modules and the submarine. The third module is a hyperbaric recompression chamber. The DDS provides a dry working environment for mission preparations. In a typical operation, the DDS hangar module will be flooded and pressurized to the surrounding sea pressure, and a large door opened to allow for launch and recovery of the vehicle. The DDS is 40 feet long, 9 feet wide, 9 feet high, and it weighs 65,000 pounds. A DDS can be transported by U.S. Air Force C-5/C-17 aircraft, rail, highway, or sealift.

The DDS is positioned aft of the submarine's sail structure, where it is connected to the submarine's aft hatch to permit movement between the submarine and the dry deck shelter. This may be accomplished while the submarine is submerged, approaching the objective area. Once the submarine has reached the insertion point, the SEALs exit the DDS and begin their infiltration. This may be ascent to the surface by deploying their CRRC or by using the SDV and traversing the distance to objective underwater.

The DDS deck captain passes notes to the SDV navigator prior to launching the SEAL Delivery Vehicle from the USS *Kamehameha*. Defense Visual Image Center

Since their deployment as combat vessels, submarines have had a close connection with clandestine operations. While the SEALs can operate over land or insert via parachute, the submarine offers them the most covert insertion platform for their high-risk missions. Here an SDV prepares to settle onto its cradle of the DDS on board the attack submarine USS *Kamehameha* (SSB-642) during training operations off the coast of Oahu, Hawaii. Defense Visual Image Center

A DDS deck captain signals to the operator of a Mark 8 SDV to move into position to be winched down for recovery onboard the nuclear-powered submarine USS *Kamehameha* (SSB-642). Nuclear-powered submarines are especially capable for this role because of their high speed, endurance, and stealth. Defense Visual Image Center

SEAL DELIVERY VEHICLE (SDV) MK8

The SEAL delivery vehicle MK 8 is a "wet" submersible, designed to carry combat swimmers and their cargo in compartments that are fully flooded. While submerged, operators and passengers are sustained by the individually worn underwater breathing apparatus (UBA). The negative aspect of this type of insertion is that when the team arrives on scene the men are soaked and, depending on the environment, either hot or cold.

Operational scenarios for the vehicle include underwater mapping and terrain exploration, location and recovery of lost or downed objects, reconnaissance missions, and limited direct-action missions.

The vehicle is propelled by an all-electric propulsion subsystem powered by rechargeable silver-zinc batteries. Buoyancy and pitch attitude are controlled by a ballast-and-trim system. Control of the SDV in both the horizontal and vertical planes is provided through a manual control stick to the rudder, elevator, and bow

The *Los Angeles*-class submarine USS *Greeneville* (SSN-772) completes sea testing for the Advance SEAL Delivery System (ASDS) off the coast of Pearl Harbor, Hawaii. The ASDS is a long-range submersible capable of delivering special operations forces for clandestine missions. The craft is a 65-foot mini-submarine that rides attached to the top of a much larger *Los Angeles*-class submarine. It has increased range, speed, and capacity over the current SDV, which is an open, wet submersible that transports SEALs in scuba gear, exposing them longer to the elements. The ASDS is operated by a crew of two and can carry eight SEALs. The vessel is connected to the host ship via a water-tight hatch and has a sophisticated sonar and hyperbaric recompression chamber. The Advanced SEAL Delivery System provides improved range, speed, payload, and habitability for the crew and a SEAL squad. U.S. Navy

planes. A computerized doppler navigation sonar displays speed, distance, heading, depth, and other piloting functions. Instruments and other electronics units are housed in dry, watertight canisters. The special modular construction provides easy removal for maintenance. Major subsystems are hull, propulsion, ballast/trim, control, auxiliary life support, navigation, communications, and docking sonar.

ADVANCED SEAL DELIVERY SYSTEM (ASDS)

Large submarines cannot always get in close to the shore to infiltrate the SEALs. This limitation forces the operators to suit up in SCUBA gear and swim to shore, launch a CRRC for a surface infiltration, or use an SDV to get to their objective. The advanced SEAL delivery system was designed to provide the SEALs with a long-range

insertion and extraction platform. The ASDS is a dry mini-submersible that can transport a SEAL squad from a host platform, either surface ship or submarine, to an objective area. No longer do the SEALs have to travel through a wet and hot, or wet and cold, environment to reach their target area. The SEALs travel in the dry comfort of the cargo/crew compartment, which gets them in place with maximum combat effectiveness. Once in position, they use the lockout chamber of the ASDS to infiltrate to their objective, a method that requires only a short duration of immersion.

A crew of two—pilot and navigator—operates the ASDS. The pilot drives the craft and is responsible for the status of ballast and trim, while the navigator monitors life support, communications, sensors, and lock-in/lock-out equipment. The battery-powered ASDS has the ability to anchor itself to the seabed while it waits for the SEALs to perform their mission. The craft has the ability to operate in both open ocean and in littoral environments.

Currently, two nuclear attack submarines (SSNs), the USS *Charlotte* and the USS *Greeneville*, based at Pearl Harbor, Hawaii, have been modified to accommodate the ASDS. Four retiring Ohio-class ballistic missile submarines (SSBM) are set to be converted to SSGN/special operations boats that will incorporate provisions to carry the SSGN (the designation for a nuclear-powered guided-missile submarine); they are the USS *Ohio,* USS *Michigan,* USS *Florida,* and USS *Georgia.*

Additionally, the new Virginia-class submarine, USS *Virginia* (SSN-774), the Navy's next generation of attack submarine, will provide the nation with the capabilities it requires to maintain its undersea supremacy well into the twenty-first century. The Virginia-class nuclear submarines will have improved stealth and sophisticated surveillance capabilities, and special-warfare enhancements that will enable it to meet the Navy's multi-mission requirements. This new design is planned to have mating capabilities to the ASDS.

The lung automatic rebreather (LAR-V) is a closed-circuit system, meaning it does not give off any telltale bubbles to compromise the swimmer. The LAR-V MK-25 provides the SEALs with enough oxygen to stay under water for up to four hours (the exact time will depend on the individual diver's rate of breathing and his depth in the water).

The term "closed-circuit oxygen rebreather" describes a specialized type of underwater breathing apparatus (UBA) in which all exhaled gas is kept within the rig. As it is exhaled, the gas is carried via the exhalation hose to an absorbent canister, through a carbon dioxide-absorbent bed, that removes the carbon dioxide by chemically reacting with it as the diver breathes. After the unused oxygen passes through the canister, the gas travels to the breathing bag, where it is available to be inhaled again by the diver.

The gas supply used in the LAR-V is pure oxygen, which prevents inert gas buildup in the diver and allows all the gas carried by the diver to be used for metabolic needs. Closed-circuit oxygen UBAs provide advantages valuable to the SEALs, including stealth infiltration, extended operating duration, and less weight than open-circuit scuba gear.

The closed-circuit oxygen UBA currently in service with the SEALs is the Draegar LAR-V MK25. The closed-circuit system prevents any exhaust bubbles from being seen on the surface of the water, thus making it easier for the team to infiltrate to their objective without being observed by enemy forces. The model is also wearing the SECUMAR TSK 2/42 life preserver, which serves as a buoyancy device, rescue unit, and lifejacket. Each side of the preserver has holders for compressed-air cylinders.

Left: **Close-up view of SEAL from SEAL Team 3 in LAR-V rebreather.**

AIR-AVIATION ASSETS

The flagship of the U.S. Air Force Special Operations Command (AFSOC), the AC-130U Spectre gunship. This highly modified gunship has gone through many evolutions from the AC-47 Spooky gunships of the Vietnam era. It is armed with a 25mm machine cannon, a 40mm Bofors cannon, and a 105mm howitzer. With a crew of thirteen, the U-model Spectre can mete out death and destruction against an enemy force as it loiters over the battle site. Its primary missions consist of close-air support, air interdiction, and force protection. This particular aircraft is in operation with the 4th Special Operations Squadron at Hurlburt Field, Florida. This gunship is deploying flares, often referred to as "angels," due to the smoke pattern they create. U.S. Air Force

The U.S. Navy SEALs are as comfortable in the air as they are in the water. Whether they are leaping off the cargo ramp of an MC-130H Combat Talon at 25,000 feet to perform a high-altitude/low-opening (HALO) jump, or descending down a woven nylon rope to perform a fast-rope insertion, the SEALs will use whatever means necessary to infiltrate into the target area.

Just as in the early days of the Vietnam War, the SEALs do not have a dedicated airlift unit assigned for their use. In Vietnam, the SEALs were inserted and extracted by the Sealords, and receive close air support from the Seawolves and the Black Ponies.

While the "air" is a prominent method of infiltration, the SEALs must call upon SOF aviation units (e.g., 160th Special Operations Aviation Regiment), or Air Force special-operations capable (AFSOC) rotary- and fixed-wing aircraft. In addition to these SOF aircraft, the SEALs may hitch a ride with other aviation assets to achieve their insertion parameters.

FIXED-WING AIRCRAFT

AC-130U SPECTRE GUNSHIP
The primary mission of the AC-130U Spectre is to deliver precision fire power and close air support for special operations and conventional ground forces. Close air support (CAS) is defined as air action against hostile targets in

A Combat Talon prepares to lift off the tarmac at Hurlburt Field. Encased in that large nose is the AN/APQ-170 multi-mode radar (MMR). Directly beneath, the forward-looking infrared (FLIR) device that allows the Talon to penetrate hostile airspace can be seen. Manufactured by Lockheed Aircraft, the Combat Talon has a wingspan of 132 feet, 7 inches, and stands at a height of 38 feet, 6 inches. This versatile aircraft is powered by four Allison turboprop T56-A15 engines that provide a thrust of 4,910 equivalent shaft power. It has a speed of 300 miles per hour and a range of 3,110 nautical miles. With the capability of mid-air refueling, the range is unlimited, providing an optimum air insertion platform for the SEALs.

close proximity to friendly forces that require detailed integration of each air mission with the fire and movement of the ground forces. The Spectre can provide accurate fire support with limited collateral damage, and it can remain on station for extended periods. These activities are normally carried out under the cover of darkness.

The lethality of this gunship is found in three weapons systems. As you enter the AC-130U, by way of the forward crew hatch and turn to your right, you will find the GAU-12/U 25mm Gatling cannon, a fully traversable weapon capable of firing 1,800 rounds per minute from altitudes of up to 12,000 feet. Positioned in the rear of the

As seen in the green glow of the night scope, members of the 16th Special Operations Wing (SOW) offload cargo and SOF personnel at a forward deployed location during a night operational mission. This MC-130 Combat Talon was part of the Joint Special Operations Aviation Component South in support of Operation Enduring Freedom. U.S. Air Force

aircraft are the 40mm Bofors gun and the 105mm howitzer. The 40mm is ideal for providing CAS at "danger-close" ranges from friendly forces, due to the small fragmentation pattern of its munitions. Alongside the Bofors is the M102 105mm howitzer, a variant of the U.S. Army's M1A1 howitzer. It has been modified to fire from an airplane by placement in a special mounting positioned in the port side of the gunship.

Unlike the "fast movers,"—F-15s, A-10s, and other jets—which must have qualified forward air controllers (FAC) for ordnance delivery in close proximity to friendly forces, the AC-130U can be controlled by fire-support officers, team leaders, or self-FAC. The fire control officers are located in the onboard battle management center (BMC). Here they man state-of-the-art sensors, navigation, and fire-control systems. These systems, when coupled with the trained eyes and skilled hands of the Spectre's officers, enable the crew to deliver awesome fire power or area saturation with surgical precision in adverse weather and in total darkness.

MC-130E/H COMBAT TALON
When their mission calls for a stealthy insertion, Navy SEALs may load up in one of AFSOC's Combat Talons. The

MC-130E Combat Talon I and the MC-130H Combat Talon II are designed for long-range clandestine or covert delivery of special-operations forces and equipment. They provide global, day, night, and adverse-weather capability to air-drop and air-land personnel and equipment in support of U.S. and allied special-operation forces.

Combat talons are equipped with forward-looking infrared (FLIR), terrain following/avoidance radars, and specialized aerial delivery equipment. Incorporated into the Talon is a fully integrated inertial navigation (IIN) system, global positioning system (GPS), and high-speed aerial delivery system. The Talons use infrared flight rules (IFR), which means the aircraft can be used in heavy ground fog or low cloud cover when the pilots cannot visually see the ground and must depend on instruments.

The special navigation and aerial delivery systems are used to locate small drop zones and deliver personnel or equipment with greater precision and at higher speeds than possible with a "vanilla" C-130. An example would be the insertion of a SEAL team operating in a sensitive or hostile territory. MC-130E/H Combat Talons are able to penetrate hostile airspace at low altitudes in order to carry out these missions. Talon crews are specially trained in night and adverse-weather operations.

HELICOPTERS

MH-53M PAVE LOW III E

The MH-53M is designed to carry out low-level, long-range, undetected ingress into denied or hostile areas. This is accomplished day or night, even under the worst weather conditions. Its FLIR, inertial GPS, Doppler navigation systems, terrain following/avoidance radar, onboard computer, and integrated advanced avionics enable it to achieve precise, low-level, long-range penetration into denied areas. The MH-53M is capable of performing day or night, in adverse weather and over hazardous terrain, and without detection while infiltrating, exfiltrating, and resupplying special-operations forces.

The MH-53M Pave Low is equipped with the interactive defensive avionics system/multi-mission advanced tactical terminal (IDAS/MATT) to provide the air crews with a heightened level of readiness and efficiency. The IDAS/MATT system is a color, multi-functional, night-vision-compatible digital map screen. Located on the helicopter's instrument panel, the display offers the crew an instant, concise view of real-time events on the battlefield. This includes the helicopter's flight path, man-made obstacles such as power lines, and even hostile threats "over the horizon."

Offering protection to the crew is armor plating as well as an assortment of weapons systems. Just aft of the flight deck are 7.62mm miniguns, and at the rear of the helicopter, on the exit ramp, is a .50-caliber heavy machine gun. While the mission of the Pave Low is primarily as an infil/exfil platform, it can also serve as a helicopter gunship.

A close-up view of a Navy SEAL as he rides to his insertion point aboard an AFSOC MH-53 Pave Low helicopter during a training exercise in the Adriatic Sea. He is wearing a ProTec helmet with military free-fall goggles. Defense Visual Information Center

CV-22 OSPREY

The Osprey is a tilt-rotor, vertical-lift aircraft that takes off like a helicopter and flies like a conventional airplane. Nevertheless, there is nothing conventional about the Osprey. Development of the Osprey began in 1981 and was originally designed for the U.S. Marine Corps under the designation MV-22. Planned for introduction into AFSOC, the special operations variant will be designated CV-22. Its mission will be to infil/exfil and resupply special-operations forces in denied or enemy areas in total darkness and in all weather

The CV-22 will differ from the MV-22 with the addition of a third seat in the cockpit for a flight engineer, and it

This newly upgraded Sikorsky MH-53M Pave Low helicopter has been modified with the interactive defense avionics system/multi-mission advance tactical terminal (IDAS/MATT). The MH-53's power is provided by two powerful General Electric T64-GE/100 engines, which provide 4,339 shaft horsepower per engine, thus allowing this 92-foot aircraft to maneuver nimbly over the battlefield. The Pave Low has a speed of 195 miles per hour and a range of 548 nautical miles, or unlimited range with aerial refueling. It is armed with any combination of three 7.62mm miniguns and .50-caliber machine guns, has a crew of six, and can easily transport two complete SEAL platoons.

U.S. Navy SEALs load into an AFSOC MH-53 Pave Low helicopter on the flight deck of the USNS *Leroy Grumman* during a search-and-seizure exercise. Defense Visual Information Center

will be fitted with a refueling probe to facilitate mid-air refueling. Additionally, the AFSOC version of the Osprey will have a modern suite of electronics, such as those installed in other AFSOC aircraft, as well as a multi-mode terrain-avoidance and terrain-following radar. To deal with the nature of special operations, the MV-22 will have enhanced electronics warfare (EW) equipment for increased battlefield awareness as well as more than 2.5 times the volume of flares and chaff, radar-jamming gear, and improved integration of defensive countermeasures. For combat search-and-rescue (CSAR), it will have an internally mounted rescue hoist and a crew door located on the starboard side of the airplane. Another significant difference between the AFSOC and Marine versions will be the fuel load; the CV-22 variant carries approximately twice as much fuel as the MV-22.

MH-60 BLACKHAWK

The 160th Special Operations Aviation Regiment (SOAR(A)) operates three Blackhawk variants. The MH-60K is a version of the Sikorsky UH-60 utility helicopter that has been modified especially for special operations missions.

These modifications include an aerial refueling capability, a sophisticated collection of aircraft survivability equipment (ASE), and improved navigation systems, all of which allow the helicopter to operate in the most austere environments and adverse weather conditions.

The MH-60K is a hybrid derivative of the field-proven UH-60A Blackhawk. The helicopter is powered by twin General Electric T700-GE-701C turboshaft engines rated at 1,700 shaft horsepower (shp) each, and an improved durability gearbox. It is aerial-refuelable in a variety of tank configurations. It has a digital automatic flight control computer with coupled automatic approach/depart/hover functions, as well as a specifically designed airframe and landing-gear features aimed at a high degree of battlefield survivability. It also features hardened flight controls with redundant electrical and hydraulic systems; a self-sealing, crash-resistant fuel system; and energy-absorbing landing gear and crew seats. With fully integrated cockpit and avionics, the MH-60K is capable of precise navigation, day or night, in all types weather conditions.

The second variant is the MH-60L, with a primary mission of carrying out inil/exfil and resupply operations in

The skill and experience of the Night Stalker pilots bring infil/exfil to a new level of excellence when coupled with the advanced integrated avionics suite—a MIL Standard 1553B data bus architecture, FLIR and radar sensors, and an air-refueling capability. The pilots of the 160th SOAR(A) are heralded as the "best helicopter pilots in the world," and they have redefined the discipline of long-range, low-level penetration.

When the mission calls for covert insertion and extraction of a team and a fast-attack vehicle at low level, day or night, in adverse weather, over any type of terrain, the Night Stalkers will fire up one of their 160th Special Operations Aviation Regiment (Airborne) SOCOM MH-47E helicopters based at Fort Campbell, Kentucky, and Hunter Army Airfield, Savannah, Georgia.

The Navy HH-60H Seahawk multi-mission helicopter is another member of the Blackhawk family. The Seahawk can undertake a wide range of missions, including logistics, combat search-and-rescue (CSAR), special warfare support, medivac, and anti-surface strike. It is fitted with an external cargo hook capable of lifting a load of more than 6,000 pounds. The HH-60H, designed for extended mission endurance and range, has a crew of four and can carry an eight-man SEAL squad. It can be armed with an assortment of weapon systems, such as a GCAL-50 machine gun; FLIR; 2.75-inch aerial rockets; and Stinger, Maverick, or Hellfire missiles. It also features an infrared jamming system, two chaff and flare dispensers, a radar-warning receiver, emergency locator, and a hover IR suppressor system. U.S. Navy

The latest Chinook is the MH-47E Dark Horsem, a heavy assault helicopter specifically designed to support SOF missions. The MH-47E is equipped with totally integrated avionics subsystems; a combination of back-up avionics architecture that includes dual mission processors, remote terminal units, multifunction displays, and display generators to improve combat survivability and mission reliability; an A/R probe for mid-air refueling; external rescue hoist; and two L714 turbine engines. The aircraft's fuel tanks are integral, replacing the internal auxiliary fuel tanks usually carried on the MH-47D. They provide 2,068 gallons of fuel with no loss of cargo space. Crewmembers for both MH-47 variants include pilot, copilot, flight engineer, and two crew chiefs.

An HH-60 prepares to insert a squad of SEALs and a Combat Rubber Raiding Craft. The Zodiac raft is attached to the underside of the helicopter. Once they have reach the insertion point, the CRRC will be released and the SEALs will helocast in after the raft.

HH-60 SEAHAWK
The Seahawk is a twin-engine helicopter in the Blackhawk family of helicopters. The primary utilization of the aircraft is for antisubmarine warfare (ASW), search-and-rescue, drug interdiction, antiship warfare, cargo lift, and special operations. The Navy's SH-60B Seahawk can be deployed aboard cruisers, destroyers, and frigates. The SH-60F is carrier-based.

An HH-60 Seahawk is used as an insertion platform for a squad of SEALs from SDV Team 2.

CH-46D helicopter, which has been in service since the Vietnam War. The MH-60S's primary missions include day/night vertical replenishment, vertical onboard delivery, airborne mine countermeasures, combat search-and-rescue, anti-surface warfare, carrier plane guard/SAR, day/night amphibious SAR, airhead operations, and special-warfare support.

MH-60S KNIGHTHAWK

The MH-60S is an integration of the U.S. Army's UH-60 Blackhawk and the Navy's HH-60 Seahawk platforms. The Knighthawk is designed to replace the aging fleet of

The MH-60S incorporates state-of-the-art technology, including the electronic flight information system glass cockpit, which integrates active-matrix liquid-crystal displays to facilitate pilot and copilot vertical and horizontal

The newest member of the Blackhawk family is the MH-60S Knighthawk, which the Navy plans as a replacement for the aging fleet of Vietnam-era CH-46 helicopters. Major differences between the SH-60 versions and the MH-60S consist of a tail wheel that sits farther aft than the current SH-60's tail wheel. This placement permits more aggressive landings in confined zones over land. The engine exhaust venting effectively reduces the aircraft's heat signature, and the cabin features doors on both sides of the aircraft, which enables rapid entry and exit during infil/exfil as well as facilitates the loading of cargo. Other features include a new glass cockpit display, which integrates the latest advancements in avionics and ergonomics by using a combined GPS and inertial system for navigation. The digital instrument array is configured to enhance the pilot's scan. The aircraft has a crew of four and can accommodate 13 passengers. U.S. Navy

situation presentations. The MH-60S also features a larger cabin than the U.S. Army Blackhawk, and its double cargo doors and an external stores support system facilitate the carrying of four external tanks. Other improvements are incorporated into the engines, rotor system, drive train, automatic blade-folding system, rotor brake, rescue hoist, automatic flight control computer, and gearbox.

The MH-60S features several modification over the HH-60 Seahawk in its role as a strike/CSAR and special-operations helicopter. The tail wheel has been positioned further aft, which allows for a steeper landing approach to a confined area; the larger cabin accommodates up to thirteen passengers; and the cargo doors are larger and on both sides of the fuselage, which allows a more rapid deployment of the CRRC used by the SEALs. The MH-60S is more crash-worthy, and it is fitted with improved self-sealing fuel tanks capable of withstanding ground fired up to 7.62mm.

The MH-60S defensive systems include a full complement of radar warning receivers, chaff and flare systems, and infrared countermeasures. Additionally, with the external stores support system, the MH-60S can be fitted with an assortment of defensive weapons systems on four forward-firing positions (e.g., M60s, M240s, GAU-17s, and GAU-1s). For more punch, it may also carry FLIR and Hellfire missiles.

INFIL/EXFIL TECHNIQUES

HALO/HAHO

There are times when, for political reasons or strategic or tactical considerations, a team cannot just drop into an enemy's backyard. The team must be inserted clandestinely from afar and outside of the nation's territorial airspace or boundaries. For such an insertion, an U.S. Special Operations team would use either high-altitude, low-opening (HALO), or high-altitude, high-opening (HAHO) techniques.

These types of parachute operations will be flights over or adjacent to the objective area from altitudes not normally associated with conventional static-line parachuting. HALO/HAHO infiltrations are normally conducted under the cover of darkness or at twilight in order to decrease the chance of observation by hostile forces. Using the ram air parachute system (RAPS), operators deploy their parachutes at a designated altitude, assemble in the air, and land together in the designated drop zone to begin their mission. This type of drop can also be conducted in adverse weather conditions.

Flying at altitudes from 25,000 to 43,000 feet mean sea level (MSL), the jump aircraft, such as a Combat Talon, will appear as a legitimate civilian airplane on an enemy's radar screens and perhaps be counted as just another commercial airliner traversing the globe. What the radar operator will not know is that the aircraft is the launching platform for the world's most lethal counterterrorism system—a team of highly trained Navy SEALs operators.

All SEALs are Airborne-qualified, earning their wings at the U.S. Army Airborne School at Fort Benning, Georgia. Once they have completed the five required jumps, they are awarded the Army's silver jump wings. An additional five jumps will qualify the operator to wear the gold jump wings of a Naval Parachutist.

High Altitude, Low Opening (HALO) parachute equipment is used by the SEALs. HALO is one of the ways teams can be inserted into denied or hostile territory. Jumpers are capable of exiting an aircraft at 25,000 feet using oxygen. They will then free-fall to a designated altitude, where they will deploy the RAPS and form up together.

Military free-fall operations are ideally adapted for the infiltration needs of Navy SEALs teams. Normal opening altitudes range from 3,500 AGL to 25,000 MSL. Depending on mission parameters, there may be some latitude given to the operators A typical team can be deployed in a fraction of the time it would take to complete a conventional static-line jump. As the AFSOC pilots approach the insertion point, the ramp of the MC-130H is lowered. With the combination of aircraft noise, the military free fall (MFF) parachutist helmet, and the oxygen mask, any normal verbal communication is almost impossible. For this reason, the team communicates by means of arm-and-hand signals, or on intra-team radios. Since he had already passed along the signals to don helmets, unfasten seat belts, and check oxygen, the jumpmaster awaits for the team to signal back "okay."

Approximately two minutes before the insertion, the jumpmaster raises his arm upward from his side to indicate that the team should "stand up." Next, he extends his arm straight out and palm-up at shoulder level, then bends it to touch his helmet, which indicates "move to the rear." The insertion team, equipped with ram air parachutes, oxygen masks, and goggles, stands up and gets ready to jump. If jumping from the side jump door, the lead man will stop a meter away; if going out the rear of the plane, the lead man will stop at the hinge of the cargo ramp. With their rucksacks or combat assault vests loaded with mission-essential equipment, the operators move toward the rear of the plane. Moments turn into an eternity, and then it is time. As the airplane reaches the proper coordinates for the drop, the jump light emits a steady green. The command is given: "Go!" In a matter of seconds, the team heads down the ramp and out into the darkness as the drone of the plane's engines fade off in the distance.

Depending on the mission parameters, they will perform a HALO or HAHO jump.

In HALO, the team will exit the plane and free-fall through the air, but meet up at a prearranged time or altitude. Jumping in this manner, the team is so small that it is virtually invisible to naked eye and it will not show up on any enemy radar screen. Using GPS units and altimeters, the team will descend until fairly close to the drop zone. At that point, the operators will open their chutes and prepare for the very short trip to the ground.

The alternate method, HAHO, also requires jumping from an extreme altitude with oxygen. The difference is that as soon as the team jumps off, the operators immediately deploy their parachutes and use them to glide into a denied area. For this type of jump, they will also utilize GPS units and altimeters. In order to maintain formation integrity, each jumper will have a strobe light on his helmet, either normal or IR, and the team members will wear the appropriate night-vision goggles (NVGs). Each man in the team will be on intra-team radio for command and control of the insertion, as well as formation on the DZ.

There are a number of advantages gained from utilization of the HALO/HAHO procedures. There are times when, due to the presence of enemy air defenses, it is the best means to infiltrate a team into a hostile area. This also increases the survivability of the support aircraft. If the mission requires the team to jump into mountainous terrain where it would not be practical or prudent to attempt a static-line parachute operation, MFF would be a practical option. Other benefits include times when navigational aids are not available to guarantee the requisite precision of drops from low altitudes (e.g., desert or jungle environments). HALO/HAHO is also employed when it is deemed necessary to land the team

Rappelling is still a viable technique utilized by the SEALs. Whether abseiling down the side of a building, or the side of a mountain, the technique offers more control than the Fast Rope Insertion/Extraction System (FRIES). Unlike the FRIES, the operator has a free hand left to facilitate firing a weapon or tossing a flash-bang grenade through a window. Here, SEALs practice rappelling from a UH-1 helicopter. Defense Visual Information Center

Fast Rope Insertion/Extraction System (FRIES). Here a team inserts from a U.S. Air Force MH-53 Pave Low. Unlike rappelling, once the trooper hits the ground, he is "free" of the rope and can begin his mission. These shooters are equipped with MP5 submachine guns. U.S. Navy

at multiple points of an objective for the purpose of attacking or seizing a primary target, and when the mission success requires a low-signature infiltration.

FAST-ROPE INSERTION SYSTEM (FRIS)

Fast-rope insertion system is a method used to insert an assault force on the ground from the air in seconds. This system begins with small woven ropes made of nylon that are then braided into a larger rope. The large rope is rolled into a deployment bag and the end is secured to the helicopter. Depending on the model of chopper, the rope might be affixed to just the outside, on the hoist mechanism of the side door; or attached to a bracket off the back ramp. Once over the insertion point, the rope is deployed and, even as it is hitting the ground, the Navy SEAL operators are jumping onto the line and sliding down as easily as a fireman slips down a pole.

As soon as the team is safely on the ground, the flight engineer or gunner (depending on the type of helicopter) will pull the safety pin and the rope will fall to the ground. Such a system is extremely useful in the rapid deployment of Navy SEALs; an entire assault team can be inserted in ten to fifteen seconds. FRIS is the most accepted way of expeditiously getting a force to the ground. Unlike rappelling, once the trooper hits the ground he is "free" of the rope and can begin his mission.

An up-close view of an actual fast rope. The rope is composed of eight strands of nylon synthetic line, and it is specially designed to facilitate the insertion of personnel from a hovering helicopter. The olive-drab rope is approximately two inches in diameter to provide ease of handling, a sure grip, and minimum stretch. It comes in 50- to 120-foot lengths, which allows SEALs to insert onto various structures and environments without the need for the helicopter to land.

Also shown here is a pair of standard-issue rappelling gloves (tan) and a pair of HellStorm heavy-duty fast-rope gloves (black) from BlackHawk Industries. The gloves incorporate a heat-barrier palm pad to protect the wearers as they insert. The glove also has a quick-release wrist cinch and a carabineer loop to attach the gloves to an assault vest or LBE.

SPECIAL PROCEDURE, INSERTION, AND EXTRACTION SYSTEM (SPIES)

The opposite of FRIS is SPIES, or special procedure, insertion, and extraction system. The Army has combined both methods into one method: fast-rope insertion and extraction system (FRIES). The Navy has maintained a separate reference to each of the methods. While fast-roping gets you down quick, there are times when you have to extract just as fast. When there is no landing zone for a helicopter, and enemy forces are closing in on their position, the SEALs turn to the SPIES method.

The SPIES technique is similar to the McGuire and STABO rigs developed during the Vietnam War. Both used multiple ropes, which often resulted in troops colliding with one another, but the latter at least had the benefit of allowing the user to employ his weapon while on the ride up. While the technique and equipment have changed, the basic methodology remains the same.

Special Procedure, Insertion, and Extraction System (SPIES). While fast-roping gets you down quick, there are times when you have to extract just as fast. A single SPIES rope is lowered from the hovering helicopter to team members wearing a special harness by which they are attached to the rope via snap links. Once they have secured themselves to the line, the helicopter whisks them out of harm's way. U.S. Navy

Mission complete! The SEALs have requested extraction and the operators lie prone in a defense perimeter awaiting the incoming helicopter. Once on scene, the Seahawk crew chief will "kick" out the SPIES rope.

Fighting the downdraft from the hovering helicopter, SEALs attach themselves to the nylon roping by means of the embedded snap links.

A bird's-eye view of a SPIES extraction. This operator is suspended from the extraction line beneath a SH-60 Seahawk helicopter, above the nuclear-powered aircraft carrier USS *Dwight D. Eisenhower.* U.S. Navy

Now a single rope is lowered from the hovering helicopter. Up to eight rings are woven and secured into the rope at approximately five-foot intervals. The operators wear special harnesses, similar to parachute harnesses, that can be attached to the rope via the rings. This is accomplished by clipping in a snap link that is affixed at the top of the SPIES harness.

Once all team members are secured, a signal is given, and the operators become "airborne" in reverse—extracted out harm's way. This method is tried and tested, and it allows the team to maintain covering fire from their weapons as they extract. Once the team has been whisked out of enemy range, an LZ is located, and the helicopter pilot sets the troops on the ground again. At this time the operators disconnect from the rope and board the chopper, which then completes the extraction.

Ready for the extraction, they close tighter and stand as the HH-60 rises higher and higher.

LAND-ASSAULT
WEAPONS

M4A1 CARBINE

In 1994 the U.S. Special Operations Command (SOCOM) adopted the M4 carbine to replace the M16A2 assault rifle and the M3 "Grease Gun." The M9 semiautomatic pistol was also selected. When selecting a weapon, operators use assorted criteria such as accuracy, range, size, weight, weight of ammo, availability of ammo, ammo capacity, rate of fire, ease of concealment, ease of maintenance, penetrating power, and so forth. As a

Above: **An M4A1 carbine erupts with fire as a patrol engages the enemy during a rehearsal. The squad will lay down suppressive fire while the radioman calls for extraction. In this case riverine boats from the SBT-22 will extract these NSW operators. Immediate-actions drills (IADs) are practiced over and over until they become second nature.**

Left: **The primary assault rifle in use with the Navy SEALs is the Colt M4A1 carbine. This shortened version of the M16A2 rifle features a collapsible stock, a flat-top upper receiver with an accessory rail, and a detachable handle/rear-aperture sight assembly. The M4A1 has a fire selection for semi- and full-automatic operation. This operator has taped two 30-round magazines together with 100 mile-per-hour tape.**

basic-issue weapon for a special operations soldier, the M4 is probably the best choice based on accuracy, range, availability of ammo, ease of maintenance, and penetrating power. Although operators are given wide latitude in the selection of primary and secondary weapons, the M4A1 is the standard-issue weapon for SEAL operators. With the advent of terrorists and other hostile persons employing body armor and bulletproof vests, it was paramount that close-quarters battle/counterterrorism (CBQ/CT) operations migrated from lower velocity 9mm rounds to the higher penetration capabilities of 5.56mm ammunition.

The M4A1, which is built by the Colt Manufacturing Company of Connecticut, is a smaller, more compact version of the full-size M16A2 infantry assault rifle; it is a weapon designed specifically for the U.S. Special Operations forces. The main difference between the standard M4 and the M4A1 is that the fire selector for the M4 can set for semiautomatic fire or three-round bursts, while the M4A1 has a fire selection for semi- or full-automatic operation. The M4A1 is designed for speed of action and light weight, which are often the needs of SEALs. The barrel has been shortened to 14.5 inches, which reduces the weight while maintaining effectiveness for quick handling in field operations. The retractable butt-stock has four intermediate stops that provide versatility in CQB without compromising shooting capabilities.

The M4A1 has a rifling twist of 1 in 7 inches, making it compatible with the full range of 5.56mm munition. Its sighting system contains dual apertures for targeting from 0 to 200 meters, and a smaller opening for engaging targets at a range of 500 to 600 meters. Selective fire controls for the M4 have eliminated the three-round burst with safe, semiautomatic, and full-automatic fire.

In addition to the CQB capabilities of the carbine, the M4A1 also provides the necessary fire power when targets must be engaged at greater ranges. In Operation Desert Storm, certain elements were equipped with suppressed 9mm rifles while performing SR missions. When one of the teams was compromised and faced a rush of oncoming Iraqi soldiers and local nomads, it was the M16s and carbines laying down a hail of 5.56mm rounds out to 600 meters that gave the team the extra edge it needed to extract from a bad situation. The same line of reasoning holds fast from the Somali experience; the M4 carbine proved to be more durable and versatile, and the 5.56mm ammunition was more lethal than the 9mm pistol round.

The lineage of the M4A1 goes back almost five decades to the mid-1950s, when the U.S. military sought a weapon to replace the heavy M14 battle rifle. That weapon, the M16, was developed in 1959 by Eugene Stoner. The lightweight Stoner assault weapon was viewed with apprehension when first introduced. Soldiers used to the heavy M1 and M14 rifles often referred to it as "the toy gun." As the Vietnam War lengthened, the M16 was modified, and in due course the XM177E1 was introduced to U.S. troops. This was a shortened version of the M16 with a collapsible stock and various barrel lengths; it was often referred to as the CAR-15. The CAR-15 saw service with the SEALs, LRRPs, SOG, and other special-operations soldiers. This carbine version of the M16 laid the groundwork for the Colt M4/M4A1 carbine in use today, which has evolved into the weapon of choice for today's special operations forces in general and Navy SEALs operators in particular.

SPECIAL OPERATIONS PECULIAR MODIFICATION M4A1 ACCESSORY KIT

The M4A1 carbine is a most capable and deadly weapon, suitable to any SEAL mission. USASOC wanted to make the weapon even more effective, whether for close-in engagements or against long-range targets. To accomplish this, USSOCOM and Crane Division, Naval Surface Warfare Center, developed the Special Operations Peculiar Modification (SOPMOD) M4A1 accessory kit, which is issued to all U.S. Special Operations forces operators.

The SOPMOD accessory kit consists of numerous components that may be attached directly on the M4A1 carbine or to the rail interface system (RIS). The various accessories provide the operator with the flexibility to choose the appropriate optics, lasers, lights, etc. dependent on mission parameters. The SOPMOD kit is constantly being reevaluated, and research is ongoing to further enhance the operability, functionality, and lethality of the M4A1 carbine. Currently, the kit is in Block 1 of a three-phase upgrade-and-modification program. SEAL operators also utilize other military and commercially off-the-shelf (COTS) modifications to enhance the M4A1 and the SOPMOD kit, depending on mission parameters, as seen in the embedded additions to the accessories below.

SPECS: M4A1 CARBINE

Caliber: 5.56mm
Weight: 5.56 pounds without magazine or 6.65 pounds with loaded 30-round magazine
Length: 33.0 inches with stock extended or 29.8 inches with stock retracted
Barrel Length: 14.5 inches
Muzzle Velocity: 3,020 feet/second with M193 round or 2,900 feet/second with M844 NATO round
Muzzle Energy: 1,113 foot-pounds with M193 round or 1,213 foot-pounds with MM855 NATO round
Maximum Effective Range: 600 meters with M193 round or 656 yards with M855/SS109 NATO round
Cyclic Rate of Fire: 700 to 950 rounds per minute
Fire Selection: semiautomatic or full automatic

SOPMOD M4

Special Operations Peculiar Modification to the M4 Carbine

Accessory Kit

Block I Accessory Kit

Reflex Sight
NSN: 1240-01-435-1916

4X Day Optical Scope
NSN: 1240-01-412-6608

Backup Iron Sight
NSN: 1005-01-449-6306

AN/PEQ-5 Carbine Visible Laser
NSN: 5860-01-439-5409

Visible Light Illuminator
NSN: 5855-01-448-5464

AN/PEQ-2 Infrared Illuminator
NSN: 5855-01-422-5253

AN/PVS-17A Mini Night Vision Sight
NSN: 5855-01-474-8904

Combat Sling Assembly
NSN: 1005-01-459-4390

Universal Pocketscope Mount (PVS14)
NSN: 5855-01-482-6164
(PVS18) NSN: 5855-01-485-7749
(M68) NSN: 5855-01-485-7755

M4A1 Carbine w/Carrying Handle
NSN: 1005-01-382-0953

Forward Handgrip
NSN: 1005-01-416-1091

Sound Suppressor Kit
NSN: 1005-01-437-0324

Grenade Launcher Mount
NSN: 1055-01-416-1090

Rail Interface System
NSN: 1005-01-416-1089

M203 9" Barrel Assembly
NSN: 1010-01-410-7422

Grenade Launcher Leaf Sight
NSN: 1010-01-418-4588

NAVSEA CRANE Surface Warfare Center Division

SOPMOD M4 Block I Accessory Kit
Special Operations Peculiar Modification to the M4 Carbine Block I Accessory Kit

Program Mission: The SOPMOD Program Management Office at NSWC Crane, IN, will provide standardized, versatile weapons accessories to meet needs across SOF mission scenarios. These accessories will increase operator survivability and lethality by enhanced weapon performance, target acquisition, signature suppression, and fire control. SOPMOD PMO will provide these accessories when they are operationally suitable, affordable, sustainable, and funded.

Program Sponsor: United States Special Operations Command
Program Manager: Naval Surface Warfare Center, Crane Division
Website: http://ssavis.socom.mil

The M4A1 with the Special Operations Peculiar Modification accessory kit (SOPMOD). The SOPMOD kit was developed by Crane Division of the Naval Surface Warfare Center for SOCOM. Crane Division continues to evaluate and refine the SOPMOD system for operators of the Special Operations Command. Department of Defense

RAIL INTERFACE SYSTEM

A rail interface system (RIS) is a notched rail system that replaces the front hand guards on the M4A1 receiver. This rail system is located on the top, bottom, and sides of the barrel; it facilitates the attachment of SOPMOD kit components on any of the four sides. The notches are numbered to make it possible to attach and reattach a given component at the same position each time it is mounted. Optical sights and night-vision devices can be mounted on the top, while top and side rails would be the choice for positioning laser-aiming devices or lights. The bottom of the RIS normally accommodates the vertical grip and/or lights. When no accessories are mounted to the RIS, plastic hand guards are emplaced to provide cover and protect the unused portions of the rail.

The Trijicon advanced combat optical gunsight (ACOG) provides increased hit potential in all lighting conditions. The exterior of the ACOG is a forged aluminum body (aircraft strength 7075 alloy). The ACOG is an internally adjustable, compact telescopic sight that uses tritium-illuminated reticles for target acquisition in all light conditions. The ACOG 4x32 model was chosen by U.S. Special Operations Command for the SOPMOD kit.

The Trijicon reflex sight is a reflex collimator sight designed for close-quarters combat (CQB). The reflex sight features an amber reticle that glows more or less brightly, depending on ambient light conditions. One of the benefits of the Trijicon reflex is that the unit operates without batteries.

Another view of the ACOG 4x32 gunsight mounted on an M4A1 carbine. U.S. Navy

ADVANCE COMBAT OPTICAL GUNSIGHT

The ACOG, manufactured by Trijicon, is the day optical scope for the SOPMOD kit. It is a 4-power telescopic sight that includes a ballistic compensating reticle. Utilizing this reticle provides increased capability to direct, identify, and hit a target to the maximum effective range of the M4A1 carbine—600 meters. As a backup, the ACOG is equipped with an iron sight for rapid close-range engagement (CRE). Both the front iron sight and the scope reticle provide target recognition and stand-off attack advantage, while retaining a close-quarters capability equivalent to the standard iron sights.

REFLEX

The Trijicon reflex sight is a reflex collimator sight designed for CQB. The Reflex sight provides a fast method for acquiring and hitting close and moving

The Comp-M sight superimposes a red dot on the target, which the brain can see, thus allowing the shooter to adjust his weapon accordingly in the fast-pace shooting environment of CQB. The Comp-M is parallax-free, which means the shooter does not have to compensate for parallax deviation. The sight may be mounted on the carrying handle or RIS of the M4A1. This SEAL has applied camo paint to the sight to blend in with the desert environment. U.S. Navy

targets, as well as engaging targets while moving. The sight utilizes a tritium-illuminated dot for use in low light and at night. Effective out to 300 meters, the Reflex sight is optimized for speed and accuracy in close-range engagements (under 50 meters) and close combat (under 200 meters) while providing the operator with a heads-up fire control during both day and night, and with night-vision equipment. The Reflex sight can be used with either night-vision goggles or in combination with a night-vision monocular, such as the AN/PVS 14. This arrangement provides a lightweight day/night capability without having to re-zero during the transition between day and night sights.

AIMPOINT COMP-M SIGHTING SYSTEM

Although not an official part of the SOPMOD kit, the Aimpoint Comp-M is often in use for CQB activities. After extensive testing, the U.S. Army adopted the Aimpoint Comp-M as its red-dot sighting system. Using a both-eyes-open and heads-up method, the shooter is able to acquire the target with excellent speed and accuracy. The Comp-M sight superimposes a red dot on the target, which the brain sees, thus allowing the soldier to adjust his weapon accordingly when facing the requirements of the fast-paced shooting environment of CBQ. The Comp-M is parallax free, which means the shooter does not have to compensate for parallax deviation. The sight may be mounted on the M4A1 carrying handle or RIS.

SPECS: COMP M

Optics: Band pass reflection coating for compatibility with night-vision equipment
Eye Relief: Unlimited
Magnification: 1X
Power Source: 2x silver-oxide or 1x lithium battery
Battery Life: 150 to 250 hours, average
Weight: 6.125 ounces with lens covers
Length: 5 inches with lens covers
Objective Diameter: 36mm
Dot Size: 3 inches at 100 yards (3 MOA)
Switch: 10 positions—8 daylight and 2 night-vision

The heads-up full rectangular view of the HDS eliminates blind spots, constricted vision, or tunnel vision normally associated with cylindrical sights. One eye looks through the sight while the other eye concentrates on the target; the brain automatically merges the two images. This proven concept affords the operator with a quick sight-on-target in both ambient and low-light levels.

The HDS is passive and gives off no signature that could be seen by opposing units using NVGs. The HDS 552 has ten NV settings, and the reticle will not "bloom" when viewed through night-vision equipment. When used in conjunction with the AN/PVS-14 night-vision device, it provides the operator with an outstanding view of the target area and immediate target acquisition even in the darkest of environments. The model M552 is submersible to one atmosphere. The pad is fitted with raised buttons, which improve the tactile feel, even with gloves.

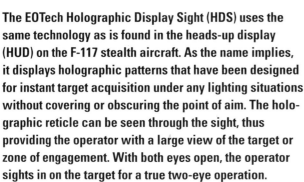

The EOTech Holographic Display Sight (HDS) uses the same technology as is found in the heads-up display (HUD) on the F-117 stealth aircraft. As the name implies, it displays holographic patterns that have been designed for instant target acquisition under any lighting situations without covering or obscuring the point of aim. The holographic reticle can be seen through the sight, thus providing the operator with a large view of the target or zone of engagement. With both eyes open, the operator sights in on the target for a true two-eye operation.

HOLOGRAPHIC DISPLAY SIGHT

Manufactured by EOTech, the holographic display sight (HDS), as the name implies, displays holographic patterns that have been designed for instant target acquisition under any lighting situation without covering or obscuring the point of aim. The holographic reticle can be seen through the sight, thus providing the operator with a large

view of the target or zone of engagement. Unlike other optics, the HDS is passive and gives off no telltale signature. The heads-up, rectangular, full view of the HDS eliminates blind spots, constricted vision, or tunnel vision normally associated with cylindrical sights. The operator sights in on the target with both eyes open.

The wide field of view of the HDS allows the operator to sight-in on the target/target area while maintaining peripheral viewing through the sight if needed, up to 35 degrees off axis. A unique feature of the HDS is that it works if the heads-up display window is obstructed by mud, snow, etc. Even if the laminated window is shattered, the sight remains fully operational, with the point of aim/impact maintained. Since many SEALs missions favor the night, it can be used in conjunction with NVG/NVD. The hallmarks of the HDS are speed and ease of use equating to incredible accuracy and instant sight-on-target operation, which can be the difference between life and death in CQB operations.

SPECS: HOLOGRAPHIC DISPLAY SIGHT

Optics: Holographic with ruggedized hood
Eye Relief: Unlimited
Magnfication: 1X
Length: 4.0 inches
Weight 6.4 ounces
Brightness Range: 28,000:1
Power Source: 2x alkaline batteries
Battery Life: 70 hours
Waterproof: 1 atmosphere
Pattern: 65 MOA outer ring with a 1-MOA dot and 8-MOA quadrant ticks
Adjustments: Elevation and windage at 0.5 MOA/click
Settings: 30 positions—20 daylight and 10 night-vision

EOTech Holographic Display Sight

Three words describe the HOLOgraphic Diffraction Sight (HDS): Fast, Fast, and *Fast!* According to EOTech's Van Donahue, "When we show these sights to the operators, they say it is FM!" FM is defined as "Trickin' Magic!" Donahue notes that Richard Marcinko, former commander and founder of SEAL Team 6, "Took one look through the sight, and said, 'This is going to save lives!'"

The HDS is unparalleled in instant target acquisition under any light situation. It is a sight without equal for close-quarters battle (CQB) operations.

The Series 500 HDS is a state-of-the-art, optical sighting system, which, for the first time, employs the use of holographic sighting technology in the small-arms and medium-caliber weapons platforms. The holographic display utilizes the same technology used in the heads-up display (HUD) of the F-117

Stealth fighter-bomber and other U.S. aircraft. When used in CQB environments, this optic provides unparalleled speed; accurate target acquisition; uncompromised use of peripheral vision; and it is passive, thus it leaves no muzzle-side signature. The M550 uses nickel-alkaline batteries, whereas the M552 uses AA batteries, which allows operators to stock, maintain, and deploy with a common battery type for their equipment.

The key attribute of the HDS is its extremely fast reticle-to-target acquisition in multiple-target situations, and in conditions where either the operator or the threat is moving rapidly. As quickly as the eyes acquire the target, the holographic reticle can be locked on. When firing a weapon using the HDS, one eye maintains focus on the target while the other eye's natural instinctive reaction places the holographic reticle on the target. The result is instant acquisition of the target for immediate and precise shot placement, without covering or obscuring the point of aim. Whether engaging a target straight on, around corners or physical obstacles, or from awkward shooting positions, the HDS makes it easy for the operator to achieve rapid reticle-to-target lock-on. Pure and simple, the HDS locks onto the target as fast as the eyes do.

The reticle pattern of the HDS is parallax-free, and the heads-up display window provides an undistorted and unrestricted view of the target scene. The HDS standard reticle image is a 65-minutes-of-angle (MOA) ring with quadrant ticks and a 1-MOA aiming dot. The holographic patterns have been designed to be instantly visible in any light, instinctive to center regardless of shooting angle, and to remain in view while sweeping the engagement zone. Mr. Donahue explained, "With thirty levels of brightness, twenty for daylight and ten for night vision, it is designed to operate in full daylight on a white target at 2:00 p.m., looking into the sun."

Other aiming reticles are available, and EOTech is working on a combination dot and M-203 sighting system.

The HDS employs a true heads-up display (HUD) that eliminates blind spots, constricted vision, or the tunnel vision associated with tubed sights. All user controls are flush to the HDS's streamlined housing, with no protruding knobs, battery compartments, or mounting rings that can block vision at the target area. True two-eyes-open shooting is realized, thus maximizing the operator's peripheral vision, and ultimately gaining greater control of the engagement zone to achieve instant threat identification. The HUD is constructed with a three-layer, shatterproof laminate glass that is a quarter-inch thick for added durability. Additional protection is provided by a "roll bar," ruggedized hood.

In holography, all the information required to reconstruct the reticle image is recorded everywhere in the HUD window. If the window is obstructed by mud, snow, rain, etc., the HDS remains fully operational, with point-of-aim/impact maintained. Even in extreme cases, such as when the laminated window is shattered, the HDS is fully functional! As long as the operator can see through any portion of the window, the entire reticle pattern is visible on the target, so that the operator can still engage with confidence.

The HDS delivers an impressive 28,000:1 bright-to-low contrast ratio. Reticles can be easily seen against white targets in desert or tundra environments—then placed in super-low-light conditions without "washing out" the target scene. For extreme low-light conditions, engaging the HDS's night-vision setting (Model 550 only) increases the contrast ratio to an incredible 28,000,000:1.

The HDS does not emit any muzzle-side position-revealing light signature, therefore the projected reticle pattern is visible only to the operator. Even Gen III night-vision equipment cannot detect a muzzle-side signature of the operator's position. All optical surfaces are flat and treated with anti-reflective coatings, which eliminate additional muzzle-side signature due to reflective glare. There is no need for glare elimination filters, which reduce the effective light transmission and further dim the target area.

Although the HDS is passive and gives off no signature, it can be used in tandem with the AN/PVS-14 Night-Vision Device. The HDS has ten NV settings, and the reticle will not "bloom" when viewed through the NVD. This arrangement provides the operator with an outstanding view of the target area and immediate target acquisition, even in the darkest environments.

Without a doubt, the EOTech HDS has no peer when the operator requires instant target acquisition in the CQB environment.

VISIBLE LIGHT ILLUMINATOR

The visible light illuminator (VLI) provides white light to facilitate movement inside darkened buildings, bunkers, tunnels, etc. The white light is useful for search and identification of targets. It has a dual-battery capability; it can be powered by three 3-volt lithium DL 123 batteries or six 1.5-volt AA batteries. The VLI is most useful in "military operations other than war," or low-intensity conflicts; when search-and-clear operations may be complicated by tripwires, booby traps, and the presence of noncombatants; and the danger of revealing one's

A SEAL on a mission in Afghanistan employs an M4A1 equipped with a Surefire Millennium vertical foregrip weapon light. This light is powered by three lithium batteries and emits 125 lumens for one hour, or 225 lumens for 20 minutes. The system shown here is attached to the RIS via an A.R.M.S. mount. The Surefire light is equipped with five distinct switches: two pressure-sensitive temporary activation pads that control the main light; a constant-on switch; a switch to lock the light in the off position for covert operations; and a third, smaller, momentary switch to control two low-output LEDs that are useful whenever there is a need for a very small amount of light (stealth navigation, night breaching operations, etc.). Department of Defense

position is offset by the need for better vision than is possible with night-vision goggles. The intense white light can overwhelm an opponent in CQB, giving the operator a momentary advantage. An IR filter can be attached to provide short-range illumination (50 meters) when using night-vision equipment. This red filter also reduces glare in smoky environments and reduces impact on the operator's night vision.

A close-up view of the Surefire 951 series weapon light on an M4. The system attaches to the rail system via a dual-thumbscrew mount. The light may be switched on momentarily by pressing the tail cap, using a pressure pad, or with an alternate on/off switch.

This SEAL has mounted a M951P Millennium Universal weapon light system onto his carbine. The M951P is powered by two lithium batteries that provide 65 lumens for one hour or 120 lumens for 20 minutes. U.S. Navy

AN/PVS14 NIGHT-VISION DEVICE

The AN/PVS-14D is the optimum night-vision monocular ensemble for special applications. The monocular, or pocket scope, can be hand-held, placed on a facemask, mounted on a helmet, or attached to a weapon. The new PVS-14D night-vision monocular offers state-of-the-art capability in a package that meets the rigorous demands of the U.S. Special Operations forces. The monocular configuration is important to shooters who want to operate with night vision while maintaining dark adaptation in the

SPECS: AN/PVS 14 NIGHT VISION

Resolution: 64 LP (minimum)
Photoresponse: 1,500 (minimum)
Signal-to-Noise: 19:1 (minimum)
Magnification: 1x to 3x
Field of View: 40 degrees
Diopter: +2-6
Weight: 13.8 ounces
Size: 4.5 inches x 2 inches x 2.5 inches
Battery: 2 AA
Battery Life: 30 hours

The AN/PVS-14D is the optimum night-vision monocular ensemble for special applications; it can be used as a pocket NVD, mounted onto a helmet, or used as a weapon sight. When coupled with a red-dot or tritium sighting system, such as the Aimpoint Comp M/ML , Trijicon ACOG system, or EOTech HDS, it provides a powerful tool for day/night operations.

opposite eye. The headmount assembly, standard in the kit, facilitates hands-free operation when helmet wear is not required. The weapon mount allows for use in a variety of applications from using sights to coupling with a red-dot or tritium sighting system such as the Aimpoint Comp M/ML, Trijicon ACOG system, and EOTech HDS. A compass is available to allow the user to view the bearing in the night-vision image.

AN/PVS-17 NIGHT-VISION SIGHT

The AN/PVS-17 is a lightweight, compact, night-vision sight that provides the operator with the capability to locate, identify, and engage targets from 20 to 300 meters. The MNVS features a wide field of view, magnified night-vision image, and illuminated reticle adjustable for windage/elevation. It can be hand-held or mounted on the weapon.

The AN/PVS-17 night-vision sight is the mini night-vision sight for the SOPMOD M4A1 carbine. This instrument incorporates a state-of-the-art OMNI V enhanced GEN III image intensification I² tube. It has a mounting attachment to interface with the Mil-std 1913 rail (RAS). The system weighs less than 2 pounds, contains a Mil-Dot reticle, and can be configured for either 2.25X or 4.5X magnification with elevation and windage adjustment.

AN/PEQ-2 INFRARED ILLUMINATOR/AIMING LASER

The AN/PEQ-2 infrared target pointer/illuminator/aiming laser (ITPIAL) allows the M4A1 to be effectively employed to 300 meters with standard-issue night-vision goggles (NVG), or is employed as a weapon-mounted night-vision device, i.e., an AN/PVS-14. The IR illuminator broadens the capabilities of the NVG in buildings, tunnels, jungle, overcast, and other low-light conditions where starlight would not be sufficient to support night vision, and it allows visibility in areas normally in shadow. At close range, a neutral density filter is used to eliminate flare around the aiming laser for improving the view of the target, for identification, and for precision aiming. This combination provides the operator with a decisive advantage over an opposing force with little or no night-vision capability. One operator commented, "When using a PEQ-2 on an M4 and PVS-7s [night vision goggles] it is like the Hand of God reaching out and taking out an individual."

The ITPIAL is a dual-beam IR laser device, used hand-held or weapon-mounted. There are seven modes of operation for aiming light and pointer/illuminator functioning individually or in combination, as well as high and low in aiming-light power. The unit is waterproof down to two atmospheres. The AN/PEQ-2, or "Pac2" as it is called, can be utilized as a laser pointer to designate a target for close air support. Note: This is not considered lasing.

AN/PEQ-5 VISIBLE LASER
The AN/PEQ-5 is a visible laser (VL) that attaches to the RIS and provides a close-range visible-laser aiming beam. The VL can be used at close range in a lighted building, in darkness with the visible-light illuminator, or at night with night-vision equipment. It is used primarily in CQB/CRE, where it provides a fast and accurate means of aiming the weapon. It is especially valuable when the operator is wearing a protective mask, firing from an

awkward position, or firing from behind cover and around corners. It permits the shooter to focus all his attention on the target while accurately directing the point of impact. Since it is visible, it can provide a non-lethal show of force that can intimidate hostile personnel by letting them know you have them in your sights.

FORWARD HANDGRIP

The forward, or vertical, handgrip attaches to the bottom of the RIS and provides added support, thus a more stable firing platform. It can be used as a monopod in a supported position, and it allows the operator to hold the weapon despite overheating. The forward handgrip can be used to push against the assault sling and stabilize the weapon with isometric tension during CQB/CRE. Using the handgrip brings the shooter's elbows in closer or tighter to his body, consequently keeping the weapon in front of the operator. It enables quicker handling when additional components have been attached to the weapon, thus providing more precise target acquisition.

A new modification to the M4A1 carbine is the redesigned, collapsible stock. The stock was designed by the Crane Division of the Naval Surface Warfare Center (NSWC) in Crane, Indiana, and is referred to as the M14 stock, or simply the Crane stock. It has been fielded by units in Afghanistan as well as in other theaters of operation.

The forward, or vertical, handgrip attaches to the bottom of the RIS. In this configuration it provides added support to give the operator a more stable firing platform. It can also serve as a monopod in a fixed shooting position.

Having numerous modifications available tends to make the shooter want to use of them all, so it is not uncommon to see an operator with as many of the SOPMOD accessories on the M4A1 as he can fit. One Special Forces operator commented that one drawback in the use of the vertical grip is the possibility it will catch on a ledge or edge of the helicopter during entry or extraction. This issue is being addressed by the evaluation of a quick-release lever on the forward grip.

The Crane stock affords the operator a larger surface for placing his cheek. This "spot weld" provides the user with a more comfortable and stable firing position than the current tubular design. The wider stock also features storage on both sides to accommodate extra batteries for such items as NVGs, flashlights, and GPS. The stock also features a rubber butt pad to eliminate slippage.

The Quick Attach/Detach (QAD) Sound Suppressor Kit MK4 MOD 0 can be quickly attached to or removed from the M4A1 carbine. With the suppressor in place, the report of the weapon is reduced by a minimum of 28 decibels (dB). The suppressor also dramatically reduces muzzle flash and blast.

CRANE STOCK

A new modification to the M4A1 carbine is the addition of a redesigned collapsible stock. The new stock was designed by the Crane Division of the Naval Surface Warfare Center (NSWC) in Crane, Indiana, and is referred to as both the M14 stock and the Crane stock. It affords the operator a larger surface for placing his cheek. This "spot weld" provides users with a more comfortable and stable firing position than the current tubular design. The wider stock also features storage on both sides that will accommodate extra batteries for such items as NVGs, flashlights, and GPS.

QUICK-ATTACH SUPRESSOR

The quick-attach/detach (QAD) sound suppressor Kit MK4 MOD0 can be quickly emplaced or removed from the M4A1 carbine. With the suppressor in place, the report of the weapon is reduced by a minimum of 28 decibels (dB). Because the 5.56mm round is supersonic, the "bang" can be heard, but it sounds more like a .22-caliber pistol than a 5.56mm (.223-caliber) round. The suppressor can buy some time while the "bad guys" are trying to figure out, "What was that? Where did it come from?" By then, the assault team should be in control of the situation. The suppressor also keeps the muzzle blast to a minimum, which assists the entry team in situation awareness. While the suppressor does not completely eliminate the sound, it does reduce the firing signature, i.e., the flash and muzzle blast. Using the suppressor is effective as a deceptive measure that interfers with the enemy's ability to locate the shooter and take immediate action. Additionally, it reduces the need for hearing protection during CQB/CRE engagements and thus improves intra-team voice communication.

BACK-UP IRON SIGHT

The back-up iron sight (BIS) provides aiming ability similar to that of the standard iron sight on the carbine, out to 300 meters. The BIS folds out of the way to allow the day optical scope or Reflex Sight and night-vision device to be mounted on the M4A1 carbine. And, in the event the optical scopes are damaged or otherwise rendered inoperable, they can be removed so BIS can be used to complete the mission. The sight can also be used to boresight or confirm zero on the reflex sight or visible laser. The BIS is manufactured by GGG and Knight Armament Company.

The combat sling affords a hassle-free, immediate, and secure technique for carrying the M4A1 carbine, especially when the weapon is equipped with assorted accessories from the kit. The combat sling can be used alone or with the mounting hardware to provide safe and ready cross-body carry or patrol carry. Whether moving in close quarters in a close-column formation or stack, the muzzle of the weapon is kept under control and does not sweep the operator or teammates around him. The weapon is carried in a ready position to immediately engage hostile targets. Although issued with the SOPMOD kit, various commercial manufacturers produce similar combat slings, and each SEAL tends to purchase or manufacture what works best for him.

COMBAT SLING

The combat sling affords a hassle-free, immediate, and secure technique for carrying the M4A1 carbine, especially when it is rigged out with assorted accessories from the kit. The combat sling can be used alone or with the mounting hardware to provide safe and ready cross-body carry or patrol carry. Whether moving in close quarters in a close-column formation or stack, the muzzle of the weapon is kept under control and does not sweep the operator or teammates around him. The weapon is carried in a ready position to immediately engage hostile targets. Although the combat sling is issued with the SOPMOD kit, various commercial manufacturers produce similar weapon slings that have also found their way into the kit bags of the SEALs.

M203 GRENADE LAUNCHER

When combined with the standard M203 grenade launcher, the quick-attach/detach M203 mount and leaf sight provide additional fire power to the operator through both point- and area-engagement capabilities. The most commonly used ammunition is the M406 40mm high-explosive dual-purpose (HEDP) projectile. This grenade has a kill radius of five meters, and it is used as an antipersonnel or anti-light armor projectile. Additional projectiles include: M381 HE; M386 HE; M397 airburst; M397A1 airburst; M433 HEDP; M441 HE; M576 buckshot; M583A1 40mm white star parachute illumination; M585 white star cluster; M651 CS gas; M661 green star cluster; M662 red star cluster; M676 yellow smoke canopy; M680 white smoke canopy; M682 red smoke canopy; M713 red ground marker; M715 green

The M203 grenade launcher is a lightweight, single-shot, breech-loaded 40mm weapon specifically designed for placement beneath the barrel of the M4A1 carbine. With a quick-release mechanism, the addition of the M203 to M4A1 carbine creates the versatility of a weapon system capable of firing both 5.56mm ammunition and an expansive range of 40mm high-explosive and special-purpose munitions.

The most commonly utilized ammunition is the M406 40mm projectile, a high-explosive, dual-purpose (HEDP) grenade with a kill radius of five meters that can be used against personnel or light armor.

ground marker; M716 yellow ground marker; M781 practice; M918 target practice; M992 infrared illuminant cartridge (IRIC); 40mm non-lethal; 40mm canister; 40mm sponge grenade (with a kill radius of five meters); and the M433 multi-purpose grenade, which in addition to the fragmentation effects is capable of penetrating steel armor plate up to two inches thick. Future development of 40mm grenades will introduce air-burst capability to provide increased lethality and bursting radius through pre fragmented, programmable HE warheads.

The quick-attach M203 combines flexibility and lethality to the individual weapon by utilizing multiple M203 setups that allow concentrated fire by bursting munitions, which are extremely useful in raids and ambushes, or the ability to illuminate or obscure the target while simultaneously delivering continuous HEDP fire. The M203 grenade leaf sight attaches to the RIS for fire control.

The receiver of the M203 is manufactured of high-strength forged aluminum alloy to provide extreme ruggedness while keeping weight to a minimum. A complete self-cocking firing mechanism, including striker, trigger, and positive safety lever, is incorporated into the receiver. This allows the M203 to be operated as an independent weapon, even if it is attached to an M16A1 or M16A2 rifle, or an M4A1 carbine. The barrel is also made of high-strength aluminum alloy. It has been shortened from 12 to 9 inches for improved balance and handling. It slides forward in the receiver to accept a round of ammunition, then slides backward to automatically lock in the closed position, ready to fire.

Carrying out their missions in small teams, SEALs depend on rapid deployment, mobility, and lethal fire power; where the emphasis is focused on "get in and get out" fast, the addition of the M203 to the team brings added punch to the already proven and outstanding M4A1 carbine.

870P MASTERKEY

The Masterkey is a Remington Model 870 Police 12-gauge shotgun that has been modified to attach to the underside of the M4A1 carbine. This attachment is well-liked for use

The Remington Model 870 Police 12-gauge shotgun has been modified for attachment to the underside of the M4A1 carbine. Referred to as the "Masterkey," it can use special breaching rounds for shooting off door hinges. It also uses normal shotgun ammunition, thus providing the operator with a formidable weapon for room clearing. Knight Manufacturing Company

Currently under consideration for addition to the SOPMOD kit is the Lightweight Shotgun System (LSS). Attachment is similar to that of the M203 40mm grenade launcher, beneath the barrel of the M4A1 carbine. The LSS is a 12-gauge weapon that most likely will be carried by the point man to provide extra punch. It would also prove useful in military operations in urban terrain (MOUT) and CQB missions. U.S. Army Special Operations Command

A group of U.S. Navy SEALs has inserted onto the fantail of the guided missile destroy underway with the Truman Battle Group during a joint task force exercise (JTFEX). At sea aboard USS *Oscar Austin* (DDG 79), the SEALs immediately take a knee to establish a security perimeter. Note that the M4 carbines have been modified to fire Simunition rounds for this exercise. U.S. Navy

This **SEAL** is armed with an **M4A1 carbine** that has been modified with the close-quarter battle receiver (CQBR), an upper receiver assembly fitted with a 10.3-inch barrel in place of the standard 14.5-inch barrel. This upper includes a replacement compensator from the **SOPMOD QD** suppressor and RAS. It can utilize all the components of the **SOPMOD** accessory kit. U.S. Navy

The **Simunition ammunition is a reduced-energy marking cartridge used for force-on-force training. The cartridge is a non-lethal round filled with a non-toxic, water-soluble detergent-based, color marking compound. The visible marking allows accurate assessment of hits. The 5.56mm rounds are accurate out to 100 feet, and also meet the needs of CQB and force-on-force training.**

in CQB operations. Using a special breaching round, the operator can blast the hinges off a door to aid in dynamic entry. It is also useful in antipersonnel engagements when loaded with buckshot rounds.

2005-2010 INTEGRATED CARBINE

The current SOPMOD kit utilizes various accessories that can be bulky, heavy, and prone to snag during movement. The integrated carbine (IC) modification concentrates on grouping these various components into a well-balanced, ergonomic, and highly reliable weapon.

The SOPMOD Block 3 upgrade will result in a more streamlined version of the M4A1 carbine, designated the Integrated Carbine. The IC design will incorporate all of the refinements for the M4A1 carbine by getting the optics and lasers *off* the weapon and *into* the weapon itself, and it will provide a thermal sighting device. Mode switches and buttons will be integrated into the vertical

A fine-tuned HK MP5 chamber in a .40-caliber S&W. This submachinegun has a safe–semi-automatic–automatic fire selector and has been modified with a Knight Manufacturing Company RIS, which allows the attachment of a Comp-M Aimpoint sight and a vertical forward grip. It is also fitted with a Knight Manufacturing Company sound suppressor.
Knight Manufacturing Company

grip to activate lasers, thermal and other sights, and visible light. The thermal sighting component might very well have the ability to be linked to JSTARS.

Modifications that might be incorporated into the evolving IC are: a visible laser component for pointing and aiming that would operate on a pulsed beam and pattern, and a visible light; a near-IR laser for aiming and pointing; a range-finding component with information sent to a display or to the weapon reticle; automatic ranging and ballistic solutions; and upgrading the enhanced combat optical sight (ECOS) with ranging information, weapon cant, barrel temperature, and shot count. All items would be readily mountable and easily removable at the operator's discretion. The ECOS would provide a balance between CQB and mid-range aiming. The sight would possess a one-power magnification for CQB and a three-four-power magnification for mid-range engagements.

Through the various iterations, modifications, and upgrades the M4A1 and SOPMOD will experience over the next decade, the M4A1 carbine will most assuredly be a state-of-the-art weapon system for twenty-first century missions. The SEALs will have more than the necessary fire power and optical capability to engage any terrorist threat or other mission parameters they may encounter.

HECHLER & KOCH SERIES WEAPONS

MP5

While the teams have transitioned to the M4A1 carbine as their primary weapon, there is still a place for the MP5 submachine gun. There are operators in the community who believe the MP5 still has a viable place in CT, CQB, and personal-protection operations. One armorer in the NSW community comments, "The MP5 will always be around."

Compact, durable, hard-hitting, and . . . all right, it is just plain sexy . . . the MP5 series of weapons remains a favorite of some shooters. For the times when you don't know which cartridge would be capable of penetrating a .75-inch (5.56mm) steel plate, the compact, concealable, and maneuverable MP5 series of sub-guns still remains a practical option. An MP5 makes sense in certain scenarios: extremely close quarters or thin walls—but even then, you would probably want a few guys on the team with the increased fire power of the M4A1. The choice of weapons will largely remain mission-dependant and thus the MP5 will remain in SEAL's armory.

Depending on the model of HK weapon, modes of fire are: safe, semiautomatic, two-round burst, three-round burst, and sustained (firing automatic as long as the trigger is held back). All MP5 versions have identical sub-assemblies, thus ensuring that many of the components of the various weapons are interchangeable within the HK weapon system. This provides the MP5 series of submachine guns exceptional flexibility to facilitate almost any mission parameter. Defense Visual Information Center

The MP5 family of submachine guns are simple to handle as well as fast and accurate when fired from the shoulder or the hip. Manufactured by Heckler & Koch (HK) in Germany, the MP5 series has become the hallmark of the CT operators worldwide. The MP5 employs the same delayed blowback-operated, roller-locked bolt system found in the proven HK G3 automatic rifle. All the characteristics of HK—reliability, ease of handling, simple maintenance, and safety—are accentuated on the MP5. Firing from the closed-bolt position during all modes of fire makes the MP5 submachine gun extremely accurate and controllable. Its high accuracy results from the fixed barrel, which is cold-forged together with the cartridge chamber. The recoil of the MP5 is extremely smooth, thus allowing the shooter to obtain highly accurate shot placement. It fires a 9mm parabellum pistol round, usually carried in a 30-round magazine and often times configured in a dual magazine holder. An operator with an MP5 can be very effective when encountering a terrorist in a hostage situation, or when engaging other mission-critical targets.

Common throughout each of the MP5 series of weapons is the capability to use interchangeable assemblies and components. This provides operators with the ability to train with one weapon to become competent with the entire weapon system.

The series also includes an accessory claw-lock scope mount and telescopic sight. HK scope mounts accommodate other scopes, such as ARMS mounts, which attach to the MP5 without any special tools at special points that ensure 100-percent return to zero.

MP5N NAVY MODEL

The MP5N Navy model was developed by HK especially for the U.S. Navy SEALs. It comes standard with an ambidextrous trigger group and threaded barrel. The MP5N fires from a closed and locked bolt in either the semiautomatic or automatic modes. This sub-gun is recoil-operated and has a unique delayed roller-locked bolt system, a retractable buttstock, a removable suppressor, and illuminating flashlight integral to the forward hand guard. The flashlight is operated by a pressure switch that is customfitted to the pistol grip. The basic configuration of this weapon makes for an ideal size, weight, and capable close-quarters battle weapon system.

MP5SD

For missions where stealth and secrecy require fully integrated sound and flash suppression, the operators may turn to the HK MP5SD model, which derives from the German *schalldampfer,* or "sound dampened." The removable sound suppressor is integrated into the MP5's design and measures up to the normal length and profile of a standard, unsuppressed submachine gun. The MP5SD uses an integral aluminum or optional wet-technology stainless steel sound suppressor. It does not require use of

Some say that S-E-F on the MP5 series trigger group stands for "Safe, Easy, and Fun," but the official HK nomenclature is composed of the first letters for the German words for "safe" (*Sicher*), "single fire/semi" (*Einzelfeuer*), and "burst/full auto" (*Feuerstoss*). Other versions of the fire selector feature a pictograph showing a single bullet in white for safe, a single bullet in red for semiautomatic, three bullets in red for three-round burst, and seven bullets in red for full automatic.

SPECS: MP5

Model:	MP5N	MP5SD3/SD6	MP5K
Caliber:	9x19 NATO	9x19 NATO	9x19 NATO
Weight:	6.47 lb.	7.63 lb.	4.40 lb.
Barrel Length:	8.85 in.	5.73 in.	4.50 in.
Overall Length:			
Stock Extended:	27.25 in.	31.69 in.	12.80 in.
Stock Retracted:	21.00 in.	25.68 in.	12.80 in.
Cyclic Rate:	800 rpm	800 rpm	900 rpm
Suppressor Length:	—	—	12 in.

MP5KA4 features three firing modes—semi, three-round burst, and full auto. Highly useful in covert missions, the MP5K can be fitted into a specially designed attaché carrying case, which allows the operator to fire the weapon while it is secured to the inside of the case. Shown here is the compact 15-round 9mm magazine, which is interchangeable with the 30-round magazine normally used with the MP5 series. Heckler and Koch

subsonic ammunition for effective sound reduction, as do most conventional sound-suppressed submachine guns. The MP5SD3 has an S-E-F trigger group, and the MP5SD6 provides a three-round burst group.

MP5K MACHINE PISTOL

The MP5K is a compact version of the M5P, referred to by HK as a *Maschinenpistole*. The "K" designation is from the German *Kurz,* for "short." The MP5K is the ultimate covert close-quarters weapon. Weighing in at only 4.4 pounds and under 13 inches in length, it is easily concealed when carried. All MP5Ks can be fitted with an optional folding buttstock. This sub-gun can be carried in a special shoulder harness for instant access and can be fired from inside a specially designed briefcase.

THE ARMORY

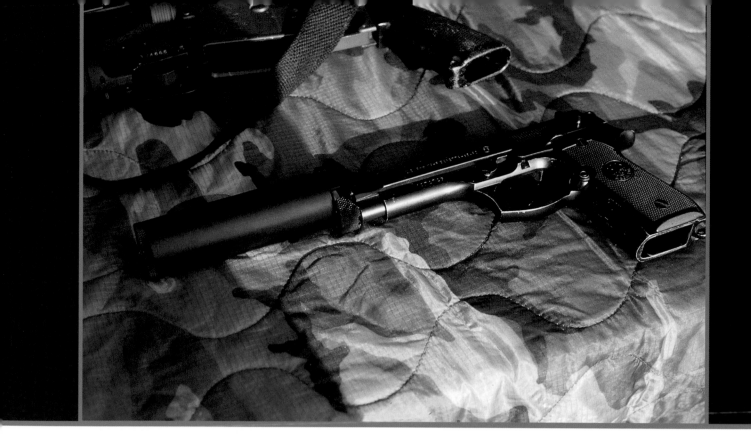

PISTOLS

The main use for the pistol is as a secondary or back-up weapon. At times, it may be employed as a primary weapon for agile and fast operations, such as a prisoner snatch or hostage situation takedown. In the mid-1980s, the U.S. military transitioned from the M1911A1 .45-caliber

Above: **The M9 was introduced as the standard-issue side arm for U.S. troops in 1985. Seen here is an M9 Beretta with a Knight Armament Company sound suppressor. The smooth cylindrical suppressor is manufactured of anodized aluminum with a steel attachment system. It weighs a mere 6 ounces and can be attached or removed in three seconds.**

Left: **Tools of the trade in this up-close and personal view are an M9 Beretta 9mm semiautomatic pistol with lanyard in a Bianchi holster, a Mk III combat dive knife, and linked 7.62mm ammunition for an M60. Today's SEAL platoon might be armed with three to four times the firepower of a World War II infantry squad. Add in the close-air support, artillery, and naval gunfire at its disposal, and a SEAL platoon is a formidable force to be taken seriously.** Defense Visual Information Center

semiautomatic pistol to the Beretta Model 92F. The Beretta utilizes the 9mm parabellum round, which is the standard NATO pistol ammunition. If the mission calls for lightweight equipment, then the Beretta or Sig Sauer pistols are among the preferred in that they provide the SEAL with twice as many rounds as a .45, usually fifteen versus eight. During missions, operators tend to carry the pistol either on a drop-down holster attached to a leg, or attached to an assault vest. Carrying the pistol on the leg allows quick access, but it can flop around and sometimes catch on ledges or edges. Wearing the pistol on the vest reverses these concerns, but then it can become tougher to access. For times when operators will be running covertly, performing site reconnaissance, or other non-descript mission profiles, they will utilize a vast array of shoulder, belt, and ankle holsters to accommodate their weapon(s) of choice.

M1911A1 .45-CALIBER PISTOL

The M1911A1 .45-caliber pistol has been in service with the military since World War I, and it still has a place in the SOF inventory today. The .45-caliber, semiautomatic pistol is a recoil-operated single-action-only hand weapon. It is a magazine-fed semiautomatic weapon, which fires one round each time the trigger is squeezed.

The M11 Sig Sauer model 228 is the standard pistol in use by the SEALs and SBT members as their standard carry pistol. The pistol is a compact version of the Sig226, 7.1 inches long and a mere 1.5 inches wide. The M11 is chambered for 9mm NATO ammunition and can be fired in both single- and double-action modes from a 13-round magazine.

The hammer must be cocked by prior action of the slide or thumbed back. The thumb safety may be activated only when the pistol is cocked. The hammer remains in the fully cocked position once the safety is activated. Over the years, five conditions of readiness for the 1911 pistol have been defined. These are: Condition 0, a round is in the chamber, the hammer is cocked, and the safety is *off*; Condition 1, referred to as "cocked and locked," a round in the chamber, the hammer is cocked, and the thumb safety is *on;* Condition 2, a round is in the chamber and the hammer is down; Condition 3, the chamber is empty, the hammer is down, and there is a full magazine in the weapon; Condition 4, the chamber is empty, the hammer is down, and no magazine is in the gun.

M9 BERETTA

The M9 is a lightweight, semiautomatic pistol manufactured by Beretta. It replaced the 1911A1 in the mid-1980s as the standard U.S. issue sidearm. It can be fired either double- or single-action and is chambered for 9mm NATO ammunition. The weapon is lighter than the M1911A1 and carries almost twice the ammunition, fifteen rounds versus eight. The ammunition is in a double-stack format, which makes the grip of the pistol wider than that of the 1911. This weapon can have the hammer lowered from the cocked, "ready to fire," position to the uncocked position without activating the trigger. This is done by placing the thumb safety on the "on" position.

M11 SIG SAUER

The SEALs, who shoot almost a thousand rounds a day, find that the 92F cannot stand up to the abuse elite warriors need to dish out, so the frogmen eventually switched to the German-made Sig Sauer line of semiautomatic pistols. They still maintain the 9mm as their caliber sidearm using the M11 Today many of the operators have transitioned to the compact M11 because it is easy to conceal.

The M11 is a 9mm recoil-operated, semiautomatic pistol introduced in 1989 by SIGARMS. It was promptly picked up as a favorite among Navy SEALs for its compact size, ease of conceivability, and accuracy.

MK23 Mod 0 SOCOM pistol was designed specifically for U.S. SOF. It is chambered for .45-caliber ACP ammunition. Although it is an exceptionally accurate handgun, there are some operators who feel the weapon is too large for normal operation parameters. In service since 1996, it was the first new .45-caliber pistol fielded by the U.S. military since the introduction of the Government Model 1911. It can still be found in the armories of the SEAL and Special Boat teams.

MK23 MOD 0 SOCOM pistol with additional LAM and suppressor. This large pistol may find its way into a SEAL's kit depending on the mission. It has also found favor among the boat skippers in the riverine force. Heckler and Koch

MK23 MOD 0 SOCOM PISTOL

The MK23 MOD 0 SOCOM pistol is a member of the HK family. It requires a tradeoff for knockdown power and accuracy, by being larger and weighing more than a Sig. Some argue that the MK23 is too large and ungainly for real-world operations, yet this weapon can still be found in the armories of the SEALs and Special Boat Teams. The HK MK23 pistol has an effective recoil-reduction system, which softens recoil forces to the components and shooter by 40 percent. It is a double/single-action pistol with a twelve-round magazine.

An innovative design feature—a high-temperature rubber O-ring on the barrel—seals the barrel in the slide until unlocking. To meet operational environmental requirements, an unlubricated pistol was tested at +160

and -60 degrees Fahrenheit and exposed to two hours of seawater at 66 feet and in surf, sand, mud, and icing conditions. A special maritime surface coating protected the pistol from any corrosion in all of these environments.

The barrel is threaded to accept attachments such as the KAC sound suppressor, and the frame is grooved to accept the laser aiming module (LAM). The weapon is aimed by 3-dot system of white self-luminous tritium dots, or the LAM. Another unique feature of the MK23 is the decocking lever. This allows the hammer to be lowered quietly, which can prove to be quite beneficial on a covert operation.

When the hammer is down, the safety lever is blocked in the fire positions, so the pistol is always ready for double-action operation. When the hammer is cocked and the safety is set to "safe," the decocker is blocked so that the pistol is ready for single-action operation by moving the safety to the "fire" position. The extended slide relapse and ambidextrous magazine release are easily actuated without adjustment of the firing grip.

LASER AIMING MODULE

The laser aiming module (LAM) is the result of more than four years of development by Insight Technology, USSOCOM, and the Naval Surface Warfare Center's Crane Division. The LAM contains visible and infrared lasers for aiming, an infrared illuminator, and a visible white light.

The current LAM model is designed to be securely attached to the MK23, utilizing the mounting grooves on the frame of the weapon. Attachment of the LAM does not affect the functionality of the weapon, and the unit can be detached and reattached to the pistol while maintaining a repeatable bore-sight of better than .4 inches at 25 meters.

The LAM can operate in one of four selected operational modes. This is accomplished by rotating the selector switch on the side of the LAM to the desired position. The four modes of operation are: visible laser only; visible laser/flashlight; infrared laser only; and infrared laser/illuminator. Once the mode has been selected, the LAM is easily activated in either a momentary or steady-on condition by depressing a switch lever located just forward of the pistol's trigger guard. Internal bore-sight adjuster's allow the LAM to be precisely zeroed to the weapon.

The current issue sound suppressor deployed by USSOCOM for the HK MK23 pistol is the .45-Cal. Suppressor manufactured by Knight Armament Company. A unique feature of this suppressor is that the operator may loosen it and index it to ten different positions. This allows the operator to adjust the weapon's point of impact to within two inches. The stainless steel suppressor is welded to five (star shaped sections) baffles, which divert the flow of gas. The KAC suppressor weighs in at one pound and can be attached to or removed from the MK23 in a matter of seconds. It requires very low maintenance and has an extremely long life. Decibels reduction is rated at 38db wet or 28db dry. Special Operations Force operators report that, with the suppressor on, all they can hear when the pistol is fired is the sound of the action.

The main use for a pistol is as a secondary or back-up weapon. At times, when the mission dictates, it may be employed for delicate or light-and-fast operations such as hostage snatch or hostage situation takedown. There have been volumes written to compare the capabilities of 9mm and .45-caliber munitions and handguns. We will not add to this debate here. In fact, while SEALs have an assortment of pistols to choose from, including the 9mm parabellum, they never officially adopted the 9mm and have opted to stay with the tired and true, hard-hitting .45-caliber weapons. Suffice to say that when it comes to handguns, special operations operators always come

SPECS: HANDGUNS

Model:	1911	M9	M11	Mk-23 MOD 0
Manufacturer:	Colt & others	Beretta	Sigarms	Heckler & Koch
Caliber:	45 ACP	9mm	9mm	45 ACP
Weight:				
w/o magazine	2.8 lbs.	2.2 lbs.	1.10 lbs.	4.22 lbs. (with suppressor)
Length:	8.6 in.	8.54 in.	7.1 in.	9.65 in. (16.56 w/suppressor)
Barrel Length:	5.0 in.	4.92 in.	3.9 in.	5.875 in.
Capacity:	7+1	15+1	13+1	12+1

back to their first love, the .45, which has been established in their minds as the best choice for CQB because of its huge knock-down power. For this reason, you will see a wide assortment of .45 semiautomatics carried by operators. Among the favorites are the Colt National Match, Wilson Combat, and Les Baer. These custom-built handguns are fine-tuned to the operator's personal preferences, so it becomes an extension of the man.

If the mission calls for lightweight equipment, then the Sig Sauer or M9 Beretta is often preferred because they provide the operator with twice as many rounds as a .45.

Operators practice these skills relentlessly to maintain their high level of expertise. Thousands of rounds will be expended to assure that, when it matters, SEAL shooters will be on the mark.

Often the weapon of choice for the entry team, the 12-gauge Remington M-870 shotgun, seen here with pistol grip, can do it all, from breaching locked doors to laying down a wall of lead shot. It is a versatile tool for CQB operations. Defense Visual Information Center

SHOTGUNS

When you think of the weapons in use by SEALs and other CT organizations around the world, images of submachine guns, assault rifles, and custom pistols first come to mind. Although less often thought of at first impulse, the combat shotgun has a key role in CT and DA missions alike.

The shotgun was used in trench combat in World War I and in close-in jungle fighting in the Pacific during World War II. Whether a pump action or semiautomatic model, it proved highly effective in laying out a devastating blast with an assortment of shot. During the Vietnam War, it was common practice among some special ops units to arm the point man with a 12-gauge shotgun.

A wide range of shotguns can be found in the hands of SEAL operators: the Remington 870, the Mossberg 500 series, and options from the Benelli series. With the trend of warfare leaning more toward the urban environment, it

The M3 is a combination pump/semiautomatic shotgun. Blending the unique features of the semiautomatic Benelli M1 shotgun with the added flexibility of a manual pump action, the M3 Super 90's type of action can be easily selected during field use by simply rotating a selector ring attached to the forearm. The semiautomatic mode on the M3 handles all standard 12-gauge shotgun shells, while the pump mode handles standard shells as well as gas grenades, flares, and non-lethal ammunition. Benelli

Here is a close look at an M60E3 as a SEAL from Team 5 prepares for a night ambush. Every fifth round is a tracer, identified by the orange tip.

MK 46 MOD 0 Light Machine Gun is the SEAL version of the M249 Squad Assault Weapon (SAW). It is a fully automatic weapon capable of being fired from prone or standing positions out to 600 meters. It is used to augment SEAL platoon firepower in concert with the MK 43 and M4A1 carbine. The weapon is chambered for 5.56mm rounds and can be fired from an M4 magazine, 100-round soft pouch, or 200-round hard box. It weighs 13 pounds and is just over 36 inches in length.

is becoming standard operating procedure to include a shotgun in a team's weapons package. Not only full-size shotguns, but specialized modifications as well, such as the 870P "Masterkey" or the SOCOM Light Shotgun System. Useful in close quarter battle, the shotgun can be set for manual breaching or antipersonnel actions.

MK46 MOD 0 LIGHT MACHINE GUN

The MK46 MOD 0 light machine gun is the SEAL version of the M249 Para SAW. The MK46 has been modified with the Rail Attachment System, which allows the attachment of SOPMOD kit accessories, such as optical sights, night-vision devices, laser designators, IR aiming devices, flashlights, and a forward pistol grip or bipod.

The MK46 is an air-cooled, belt-fed, gas-operated automatic weapon that fires from the open-bolt position. It has a cyclic rate of 750 rounds per minute. This M249 mod is fitted with an AN/PVS14 night-vision optic and a 30-round M16 magazine is in place rather than the 200-round box magazine.

M60 MACHINE GUN

The M60 series of machine guns has been in service since the 1960s. It was introduced as a crew-served weapon, but over the years the SEALs have modified the system, and a

When you have to have suppressive fire, and you need a lot of it, the MK 43 MOD 0 is the perfect choice. Although the design is more than forty years old, the M60 has undergone numerous modifications, including shortening the weapon and adding a forward grip. It was introduced as a crew-served weapon, but an experienced operator can accurately fire from the shoulder. This veteran firearm still has a home among the SEALs, who are seen here during a joint CSAR exercise in Fallon, Nevada. U.S. Navy

After extensive testing, the M240, manufactured by Fabrique Nationale, was selected as the replacement for the aging M60 machine gun. The highly reliable M240 7.62mm machine gun delivers more energy to the target than the smaller caliber M249 Squad Assault Weapon (SAW). It has an effective range of 1.1 miles with a cyclic rate of fire of 650 to 950 rounds per minute.

The M14 rifle was the standard service rifle until it was replaced in the late 1960s by the M16A1 rifle. Yet, the M14 remains the weapon of choice for some U.S. SOF operators. The Navy SEALs continue to maintain this rifle in their inventory due to the solid take-down capabilities of its 7.62mm round. Here, a SEAL armed with an M14 waits semi-submerged at an ambush site. He has inflated his UDT vest to keep his head just above the surface of the water.
Defense Visual Information Center

single man now operates the machine gun. The M60E3 is a lightweight, gas-operated, air-cooled, disintegrating metallic link-belt fed 7.62mm machine gun. Modified from the standard M60, the M60E3 has a receiver-attached bipod that easily deploys for stability. It has an ambidextrous safety, universal sling attachments, a carrying handle on the barrel, and a simplified gas system.

The MK43 MOD 0 machine gun is a further product enhancement of the M60E3 for the SEALs. It is a gas-operated, fully automatic, link-belt-fed machine gun that fires from an open bolt and has a quick-change barrel.

The M14 is a gas-operated semiautomatic rifle in use with the SEALs. It has a heavy match-quality barrel of 22 inches, giving it an overall length of 44.3 inches. It is fitted with either a wood or fiberglass stock and employs a 20-round magazine. The rifle has an effective range out to 400 meters with a rate of fire of 750 rounds per minute.
Defense Visual Information Center

M240 MACHINE GUN

After extensive testing, the Fabrique Nationale (FN) M240 was selected as the replacement for the aging M60 machine gun system. This highly reliable 7.62mm machine gun delivers more energy to the target than the smaller caliber, M249 squad assault weapon (SAW). It has an effective range of 1.1 miles, with a cyclic rate of fire of 650 to 950 rounds per minute controlled by three different regulator settings. The M240G is modified for ground use by the installation of an "infantry modification kit," comprising a flash suppressor, front sight, carrying handle for the barrel, buttstock, infantry-length pistol grip, bipod, and rear-sight assembly. While the weapon posseses some of the basic characteristics of the M60, the M240 series is an improvement in reliability and maintainability over the older M60.

M14 RIFLE

The M14 is a gas-operated semiautomatic 7.62mm (.30-caliber) rifle currently in use with the SEALs. It has a heavy match-quality barrel of 22 inches that results in an overall length of 44.3 inches. It is fitted in either a wood or fiberglass stock, and deploys a 20-round magazine. The rifle has an effective range well beyond 500 meters at a rate of 750 rounds per minute. The M14 rifle was the standard service rifle until it was replaced in the late 1960s by the M16A1 rifle, but the M14 nevertheless has found a home among a few SOF operators. The Navy SEALs continue to maintain this rifle in their inventory due to the solid takedown capabilities of the 7.62mm round.

M91 SNIPER RIFLE

The M91 is a bolt-action 7.62mm sniper rifle developed for the SEALs by Crane. It is based on the Remington 700 series, which is analogous to the sniper rifles of the other services. It has a Remington trigger with a 1 in 11.2 twist chrome-moly barrel, which is free floating in an HS Precision fiberglass stock. The M91 is issued with a Leupold 10-power scope and a Harris bipod, and is rated at 1 MOA accuracy.

In addition to the M91, the SEALs field the .300 WinMag sniper rifle manufactured by NSWC Crane. It too is a bolt action rifle based on the Remington 700 action.

MK11 RIFLE SYSTEM

The MK11 MOD 0 Type rifle system 7.62mm is fabricated by Knight Manufacturing Company, Florida. It is a highly accurate, precision semiautomatic sniper rifle chamber capable of delivering its 7.62mm round well out to 1,000 yards. With a half-inch MOA accuracy, the MK11 has won acceptance in the SOF community as one of the finest semiautomatic sniper rifles in the world.

The MK11 is based on the original SR25, and appears to be an M16 on steroids. In fact, 60 percent of the parts are common with the M16 family. If an operator is familiar with the M16 or M4A1, his hands will naturally fall in place on the MK11. From the pistol grip to the safety switch or magazine release, it operates like an M16 or M4A1. The result of this replication is a rifle that is quicker to assimilate, easier to maintain, and more seamless in transition than any other semiautomatic 7.62mm rifle in the world.

While the SOPMOD kit contains the M203 grenade launcher, the Vietnam-era M79, which fires the same 40mm grenade as the M203, can still be found in the armories of many SOF units. Similar to the M4 accessory, it is a single-shot, breech-loading weapon. Unlike the M203, the weapon breaks open rather than slides forward, allowing what many believe to be a quicker method of loading. It has an open, fixed front sight and an open, adjustable rear sight. Many in the spec ops community also consider it to be more accurate than the M203.

The MK11 MOD 0 Type Rifle System 7.62mm is produced by Knight Manufacturing Company. It is a highly accurate, precision semiautomatic sniper rifle chambered to deliver a 7.62mm round well out to 1,000 yards. With a half-inch MOA accuracy, the MK11 has won acceptance in the special operations forces community as one of the finest semiautomatic sniper rifles in the world. Knight Manufacturing Company/Ichiro Nagata

As with the M4A1, the MK11 has two main sections: the upper and the lower receiver. This allows for cleaning in the manner troops have been familiar with since basic training. Another benefit of the receiver's breakdown is the fact that the rifle may be transported in a smaller package for clandestine activities. Once on target, the rifle is merely reassembled with no affect on the zero of the optics.

The MK11 MOD 0 system includes a free-floating 20-inch barrel and a free-floating rail adapter system (RAS). The RAS is similar to the RIS on the M4A1. Another feature of the SR25 is the ability to mount a sound suppresser. The muzzle blast becomes negligible, and the only sound heard is the sonic crack of the round going down range.

HEAVY SNIPER RIFLES–THE .50S

When the mission calls for a hard-target interdiction (HTI) at very long range—more than 1,000 meters—the SEALs will turn to the *big* guns. HTI would entail taking out such targets as a generator or an airplane, helicopter, or vehicle.

The M82A1 is a one-man, portable, semiautomatic rifle with a magazine holding up to ten rounds of .50-caliber Browning machine gun (BMG) ammunition. Another "fifty" common in the armory is the bolt-action TAC-50 from McMillian, which is fine-tuned by NSW armorers.

ANTITANK

AT4 LIGHT ANTITANK WEAPON

The M136 AT4, the U.S. Army's principal light antitank weapon, provides precision delivery of an 84mm, high-explosive, antiarmor warhead with negligible recoil. The M136 AT4 is a man-portable, self-contained, antiarmor weapon consisting of a free-flight, fin-stabilized, rocket-type cartridge packed in an expendable, one-piece, fiberglass-wrapped tube. Unlike the older M72 LAAW, the AT4 launcher does not need to be extended before firing.

To engage hard targets at distances greater than 1,000 meters, the SEAL may use the Barrett M82A1 semiautomatic .50-caliber rifle, which is particularly useful against light vehicles and aircraft.

When the warhead makes impact with the target, the nosecone crushes and the impact sensor activates the internal fuse. Upon ignition, the piezoelectric fuse element triggers the detonator, thus initiating the main charge. This results in penetration where the main charge fires, and it sends the warhead body into a directional gas jet that is capable of penetrating more than 17 inches of armor plate. The aftereffects are "spalling," the projection of fragments, incendiary effects that generate blinding light, and obliteration of the target's interior.

KNIVES

As with sidearms, SEAL operators have wide latitude as to what knife they carry. But find two SEALs who have purchased the same knife and it is immediately marketed as the "official SEAL knife." A wide assortment of edged weapons can be found among the teams, from Ka-Bars

The M136 AT4 is a lightweight, self-contained, man-portable, antiarmor weapon. Inside of the expendable, one-piece fiberglass-wrapped tube is a free-flight, fin-stabilized, rocket-type cartridge. The launcher being fired here by an Army SOF operator is watertight for ease of transportation and storage. Unlike the M72-series LAAW, the AT4 launcher does not need to be extended before firing. With a range of 2,100 meters, the warhead is capable of penetrating 400mm of rolled homogenous armor.

SEALs have wide latitude in the selection of knives. Shown here is a member of SEAL Team 3 with a commercial, over-the-counter (COTS) dive knife. He has affixed a smoke/flare to the scabbard with 100-mile-per-hour tape.

The Buck 184 "Buckmaster" is a large Bowie-bladed survival knife developed at the request of the Naval Special Warfare Command for use by SEALs. It has a 7.63-inch blade and an overall length of 12.56 inches. The handle is hollow to allow storage of survival or mission items. The two pins, which are removable, can serve as an improvised grappling hook. The scabbard also features a small pouch with a compass. Although the Buckmaster is a substantial survival or field knife, many operators find it too cumbersome and heavy.

The operator is carrying the 21st Century Ka-Bar fighting/utility knife. The new Ka-Bar has a blade of high-carbon, high-chromium, cold-rolled stainless steel 7 inches in length. The overall knife is 12 inches. The handle is molded Kraton-G thermoplastic for high resistance to chemical and environmental conditions. The knife is carried in a custom-molded Kydex sheath that securely holds it in place with a snap closure.

The SEAL 2000 SOG knife is a weapon of choice for many SEAL operators. It features a 7-inch blade and overall length of 12.25 inches. The knife has a Zytel plastic handle with diamond pattern to provide a sure grip even when wet. It comes with a Kydex sheath.

The SOG SEAL Pup is a smaller, more manageable version of the SEAL 2000 knife. The partially serrated blade is 4.75 inches, the overall length is 9 inches, and it weighs a mere 5 ounces. It comes with a standard-issue jump-rated Kydex scabbard but is shown here with a specially produced nylon cordura scabbard with accessory pouch for such items as a Leatherman or Swiss Army knife, compass, or other items.

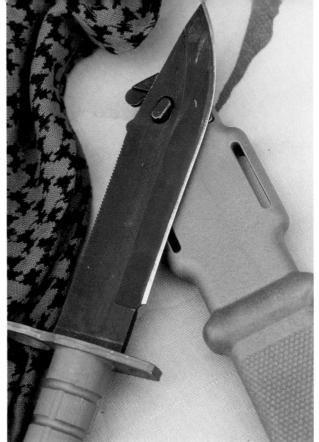

The M9 bayonet is the U.S. Army standard-issue bayonet, compatible and interchangeable with prior designs. Using bayonet lugs, the M9 mounts on the M16A1, M16A2, M4, and M4A1. It features a 7.125-inch blade, modified wire-cutter, T-lug, and blade stop. The blade can be inserted into the scabbard facing either direction, and the scabbard has easy attachment/removal from a belt. The M9 has a black oxide blade coating, a weather-resistant, zinc-phosphate coating on all metal hilt parts and a Zytel plastic handle. This SEAL has attached a combination smoke/flare to the scabbard.

The M9 bayonet has a slot located near the end of the blade that allows the bayonet to mate with the scabbard. In this configuration, the operator can use the M9 as a wire cutter.

and standard-issue MK 3 dive knives to the heavy-duty Buck master, Glock Field Knife, SOG SEAL 2000, or SEAL Pup. From the steamy jungles of the Rung Sat Special Zone in Vietnam to the wasteland of Iraq during Operation Iraqi Freedom, these knives have accompanied many a Navy SEAL on a deadly mission.

Selection of an edged weapon is as personal and different as the operators themselves, and a wide assortment are found with new and old blade designs. The standard M9 bayonet, the latest in custom-made combat knives, folding knives from Spyderco and Emerson, and even pocket tools such as the Leatherman can be found in the operator's duffel, LBE, assault vest, or kit bag. The Navy SEAL is as comfortable—and as lethal—with a knife as he is with any firearm.

From crimping a blasting cap to "det cord" or attaching a "PAK4" to an M4A1, prying the lid off a demolitions container, or chopping ice for a rum and Coke, this multi-purpose pocket "tool kit" provides a plethora of uses. An offshoot of the well-known "Swiss Army knife," these tools are available from a wide assortment of manufacturers. Seen here is the Leatherman Wave, which incorporates pliers, knives, screwdrivers, saw blades, and other useful accoutrements.

DEMOLITIONS

Due to the nature of their missions, Navy SEALs use a vast array of demolitions. From small charges to blow a lock off a door to larger charges to take down bridges, they have the munitions, techniques, and experience to accomplish any mission profile. SEAL demolitions specialists maintain volumes of data on the most expedient method of employing explosives. How do you blow off a wooden door or a metal door from a frame building? From a concrete bunker? Listing all the explosive and detonation devices would cover volumes, so what follows is a sampling of the munitions in use with the SEALs.

The M18A1 mine, more commonly referred to as the Claymore mine, is primarily employed as a defensive antipersonnel weapon, but it has been known to be employed in certain offensive situations. The M18A1 can be deployed as a mine, an offensive weapon, or a booby trap, and it also has its uses as a pursuit deterrence device. Additionally, the Claymore has the capability of being sighted directionally to provide fragmentation over a specific target area, and it can be command detonated.

A silhouette target placed 50 meters in front of an exploded Claymore antipersonnel mine displays some of the damage inflicted by the 700 steel ball bearings released by the mine upon detonation. Department of Defense

The M18A1 antipersonnel mine is a curved, rectangular plastic case that contains a layer of composition C3 explosive. Packed into the explosive are 700 steel balls. The front face, which contains the steel balls, is designed to produce an arc-shaped spray that can be aimed at a predetermined target area. It comes in a bandoleer that includes the M18A1 mine, an M57 firing device, an M40 test set, and an electrical blasting-cap assembly.

The M112 block demolition charge consists of 1.25-pounds of composition C4 explosive packed into an olive-drab Mylar-film container with a pressure-sensitive adhesive tape on one surface. A peelable paper cover protects the tape. Composition C4 is white with a unique

The M18 Claymore spreads a fan-shaped pattern of steel balls in a 60-degree horizontal arc at a maximum height of 2 meters and covers a casualty radius of 100 meters to an optimum effective range of 50 meters. The forward danger radius for friendly forces is 250 meters. The back-blast area is unsafe in unprotected areas 16 meters to the rear and sides of the munition. It measures 8.5 inches long, 1.375 inches wide, 3.25 inches high, and it weighs 3.5 pounds.

M112 block demolition charge is used for an assortment of demolition work. It consists of 1.25 pounds of composition C4, a white explosive packed in an olive-drab Mylar-film container that aids in concealing the explosive. The M112 block-demolition charge can be cut and molded to fit irregularly shaped targets and is easily attached to the target.

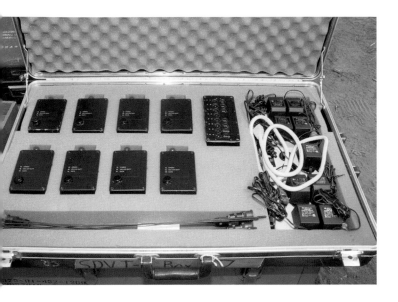

The MK 186 Radio Firing Device (RFD) kit contains one transmitter, eight receivers with antennas, and battery chargers in a hard-shell carrying case. The MK 186 system is an intelligent and discrete two-way radio-controlled demolition initiation system. The RFD incorporates state-of-the-art microprocessor and encryption technology to provide the operators with a reliable, accurate initiation device that is also compact and safe. Each receiver has the capacity to initiate at least eight M6 electric blasting caps.

lemon-citrus smell. M112 block demolition charges are used primarily for cutting and breaching all types of barriers and structures. Because of its malleability, the charge is perfectly appropriate for cutting irregularly shaped targets such as steel and steel beams. The adhesive backing allows the charge to be attached to any relatively flat, clean, dry surface that is above the freezing point.

Explosive Breaching covers a diverse selection of explosives and techniques. Explosives such as flexible linear charges, detonation-cord ("det-cord"), and composition C4 are all to be found in this demolitions array. A common technique used is the silhouette charge; a cardboard silhouette with one to three warps of det-cord around the perimeter will do a good job of cutting through a door. By replacing the det-cord with the proper amount of C4, the silhouette will now blow out a substantial passageway through a cinder-block wall.

Specialty demolitions called plastic-bonded explosives (PBX) are available to covert warriors in an assortment of packages. Plastic-bonded sheet explosives are manufactured with RDX or PETN. These are adaptable, bendable sheet material. Various types of ribbon PBX are available;

one type is for breaching doors and windows, and a pliable tape with metal cladding forms a linear-shaped charge that can be used for cutting holes in brick and other masonry walls. Other explosives not normally used by conventional forces include an explosive charge that provides instantaneous breaching through multiple layers of block walls.

The SEAL operator is trained to breach every barrier, from wooden frame to reinforced steel doors.

FAST-ATTACK VEHICLE

Fast-attack vehicles (FAVs) were first introduced into military service in 1980 with the U.S. Army's 9th Light Infantry Division. In the mid-1980s, the U.S. Special Operations forces took delivery of a number of the FAVs and, as one of the operators commented, "We began to tinker with them." Today this modified dune buggy, which now is fitted for three men, is officially called the desert patrol vehicle (DPV) or light strike vehicle, but it is still referred to as the FAV.

The frame is polyfiber and the cowling can be removed dependent upon the mission profile. Baskets alongside the frame provide storage for food, water, ammunition, and individual's gear. Collapsible fuel bladders can also be mounted in the baskets, thus providing the DPV an extended range for special missions. In support of combat search-and-rescue operations, the baskets can be used for the recovery of two downed pilots.

The Desert Storm-era DPVs had a Volkswagen-style four-speed transmission, but it is as much a VW as the late Dale Earnhardt's car was a Chevy. The transmission has been highly modified, and only reverse is stock—because no one manufactures a *racing* reverse gear.

The engine is a 4-cylinder, air-cooled motor, which in the current model is manufactured by Porsche. It also has an internal/external oil cooler on it, which is a big improvement over the FAVs used in Desert Storm. With the new oil cooler the DPVs can run in 120-degree-plus weather, wide open and with no problems. The air cleaner is a two-stage system. No matter what conditions it is running in, the first stage stops all the dirt; the crews have never been able to get any dirt out of the second stage.

The DPV has skip plate all along the bottom, so rocks and pebbles don't have an effect on the crew or the vehicle. Clearance is approximately 16 inches with wheel travel of 24 inches. It has four shock absorbers in the rear, of which three are working all the time. The fourth is the secondary. When the rear wheel travels so far, it will engage an additional set of torsion bars and the fourth shock.

The DPV is a three-man vehicle used for many types of long-range desert operations, including close air support (CAS) or combat search-and-rescue (CSAR). It has a two-stage independent suspension all the way around, and four-wheel disc brakes. On the front end is the top of the coil spring, which is working all the time. Once this coil is depressed to a predetermined degree, the secondary coil kicks in to ensure a smooth ride throughout the entire range of motion.

A U.S. Navy SEAL performs live-fire target-shooting exercises from the back seat of a DPV. He is using an M2 .50-caliber heavy machine gun with an AN/PEQ-2 IR laser pointer, used for nocturnal missions. In the foreground is a light antiarmor weapon. The SEALs have brought the DPVs out of storage to help them engage in America's Global War on Terrorism. U.S. Navy

A view from inside a SEAL Team 3 DPV during a training exercise at the Naval Amphibious Base. Lieutenant Junior Grade Thomas Chaby (right) and Hospital Corpsman First Class Joe Pappamihiel have access to an arsenal of weapons, including the Browning .50-caliber heavy machine gun and the MK19 40mm grenade launcher. Mission Roles: direct action, special reconnaissance, combat search-and-rescue, weapons platform. Defense Visual Information Center

The entire vehicle is tunable by the crew to coincide with the mission, load, and terrain. The DPV can be set up to carry 2,000 pounds of gear. The seats feature a five-point harness, so the tighter the operator straps himself in, the better he feels. He won't get knocked around much.

The tires are Mickey Thompsons with bead lock. This allows the DPV to run even on tires that are flat without the tires coming off the rims. The sidewall also features a tread pattern so that whether they are flat or not, they have traction. Along with the disc brakes, the DPV features cutting brakes. By operating levers, the driver can brake the vehicle and place it in a sharp turn. This is extremely useful in an ambush, when the driver needs to maneuver the DPV to get armament lined up on the enemy.

The DPV bristles with hard points to mount and support various weapons systems. There are two racks for AT4 antitank missiles, and additional AT4s can be carried in the side baskets. There is also room in the baskets for Stinger shoulder-launched surface-to-air missiles. The top mount will accept an M2 .50-caliber heavy machine gun or a MK19 40mm grenade launcher. The front mount for the operator riding "shotgun" normally accepts a 7.62mm light machine gun. Additional MK19s can be mounted on the vehicle, which gives the crew substantial fire power. In fact, with MK19s mounted both top and front, the DPV crew can put more than 180 40mm rounds down range in less than thirty seconds, a technique often referred to as "steel rain." There is also a rear mount for an M60A3 or other light machine gun. The primary use for this rear weapon is to break contact with enemy forces.

SPECS: DESERT PATROL VEHICLE

Description: 3-man 2 x 4

Gross DPV weight: 3,500 pounds

Wheelbase: 114 inches

Overall length: 161 inches

Overall height: 79 inches

Overall width: 83 inches

Ground clearance: 16 inches

Maximum grade: 75 percent

Maximum side slope: 50 percent

Acceleration: 0 to 30 miles per hour in 4 seconds

ADVANCED LIGHT STRIKE VEHICLE

The advanced light strike vehicle (ALSV) is the next progression in the Chenowth family of fast attack vehicles. The high-performance, all-terrain vehicle is designed to infiltrate, survive, and exfiltrate on terrain across the earth as the SEALs take their place in the Global War on Terrorism. From the wastelands of Afghanistan to the urban areas of Iraq, ALSVs can traverse virtually any terrain with unmatched agility and speed. The vehicle will support two to four operators, depending on the mission parameters.

The newest generation of ALSVs includes several major improvements to fire power and mobility, including a main weapons station with 360-degree traverse and coverage, plus a wide assortment of weaponry including accommodation for an M2 .50-caliber heavy machine gun or a MK19 40mm grenade machine gun. Utilizing remote control and stabilized platforms, the ASLV can deliver accurate shoot-on-the-move lethality. All-wheel drive, an advanced diesel engine by Porsche, and power steering are now standard equipment.

TACTICAL GEAR

LOAD-BEARING EQUIPMENT
HARNESSES AND ASSAULT VESTS

It began with stuffing extra magazines into BDU pockets, then into spare ammo pouches. As more specialized equipment was added, new load-bearing equipment (LBE) harnesses and assault vests were incorporated into the unit's kit bag. Today, depending on the mission, the most common way of carrying gear is on an assault vest or chest harness.

Above: **The delta operator's assault vest (DOAV) manufactured by BlackHawk Industries features pouches to hold magazines for the weapon of choice for the mission. Smaller pockets and pouches are accessible for pistol magazines, shotgun shells, flex cuffs, strobes, chemlights, first-aid pressure dressings, and grenades (smoke, stun, CS gas, and frags). The DOAV also has internal pockets for storage of maps and other equipment.**

Left: **Intra-team communications is essential to a successful operation. The pliable rubber ear cup establishes contact with the operator's head to quell ambient sounds. The headset has an adjustable elastic strap to allow the user to comfortably wear the device whether fast-roping, moving under fire, or even swimming. The unit is sealed for use in the water.**

Attached to the pistol belt, an assault vest provides easy access to ammunition and other items during the fast-paced CQB mission. Pouches on the front of the vest hold magazines for M4A1s, MP5s, or other weapons. Small pockets and pouches are readily available to accommodate pistol magazines, shotgun shells, first-aid field dressings, flex cuffs, strobes, chemlights, pressure dressings, or grenades. Some vest designs are of a modular nature, where the vest itself is made up of attachment points of Velcro, Alice clips, or other fasteners. These systems allow for modification with assorted holsters, magazine pouches, radio pockets, etc. Internal pockets allow the operators to stow maps or other gear. And these vests might have various back pouches to accommodate such items as gas masks, helmets, demolition equipment, and other mission-essential items.

Recently, as seen in Operation Enduring Freedom and Operation Iraqi Freedom, many SOF operators including SEALs are gravitating to the chest harness. A number of manufacturers offer COTS harnesses—Blackhawk Industries, High Speed Gear, and Eagle, among others. The larger pouches available can accommodate two or three M4 30-round magazines, depending on the manufacturer. And other pockets are large enough for radios, MREs, compass, or other mission-essential gear. The operator may also place a one-quart canteen in the large rear compartment of the harness.

The vest features two cavernous back pouches to accommodate such items as gas mask, helmet, demolitions equipment, and other mission-essential items.

SOP will determine the layout of the mission-essential gear for "like-teams," entry teams, breaching teams, clearing teams, sniper teams, and so forth. All team members are sure of each member's equipment capabilities, equipment is exchangeable, training continuity is achievable, and less variation in team equipment means fewer problems to consider. Another requisite item worn on the vests will be the American Flag.

Assault vests, like this one manufactured by Eagle Industries, are commonly used by SEALs. The vests allow the operators to keep necessary tactical equipment within reach at a moment's notice, when seconds can mean the difference between life and death. Attached to the pistol belt, the assault vest provides easy access to ammunition and other items during a fast-paced CQB mission.

The Denali Chest Harness, manufactured by High Speed Gear, can carry a CRRC load of gear for any SEAL operation. The main pouches accommodate twelve 30-round M4 magazines, and the smaller pouch on each end can hold a 2-quart canteen, a 50-ounce hydration bladder, or blow-out kit. Sewn onto each end pouch are smaller pouches for four pistol magazines, four fragmentation grenades, and two smoke grenades. Atop the harness is a horizontal pouch, which can accommodate such items as a Saber radio, compass, or strobes. Affixed to this pouch are pace-counting beads. On the rear of the harness are four large mesh pockets. The main body unzips to reveal a map case with assorted pockets. At the bottom of the harness is a removable, tubular pouch that will accommodate such items as sling rope or a poncho. The harness can be worn on the back for exceptional load balancing while humping the boonies, then turn around for easy access of gear once on-site.

Shown here is the Commando Chest Harness from BlackHawk Industries. This harness has four main pouches big enough for up to three M4 or two M14 magazines, or sixteen 40mm grenades. To aid in stealth, each pouch has a divider to prevent the magazines from slapping together. The two end utility pouches can hold numerous other items, such as radios, MREs, compass, and strobe. The inside back portion is padded with quarter-inch closed-cell foam that provides the wearer with comfort as well as added flotation when crossing rivers or streams. In addition, there is a large utility or map pocket. It is fitted with a quick-release waist strap and belt-loop attachment system.

Whether used for protection from the elements, blast, or debris, or as camouflage, the SEALs use a wide assortment of gloves appropriate to the tasks.

From left to right:

The Nomex Flight Glove has been a favorite with the SEALs since Vietnam. It is lightweight with a soft cowhide palm that allows for a tactile sense while providing protection to the wearer. Operators will often cut off the tip of the index finger so nothing interferes with the operation of the trigger. The glove is heat-resistant to 900 degrees Fahrenheit.

The operator's glove, manufactured by Hatch, is of Kevlar construction that provides four times the cut-resistance of leather. The palms of the glove feature kangaroo leather to give the wearer superb manual dexterity. The glove also has a long-gauntlet design to provide additional coverage of the forearm. Since many operators cut off the fingertip anyway, the Hatch glove features cut-ring stitching to allow removal of the glove's index finger for trigger control, while preventing the finger from becoming unraveled. The operator model is heat-resistant to 800 degrees Fahrenheit.

The HellStorm S.O.L.A.G. (Special Operations Light Assault Glove) from BlackHawk Industries is made of advanced synthetic composite materials. It is breathable, quick drying, lightweight, and maintains excellent dexterity. The S.O.L.A.G. glove also features quad-stitch lines on the index finger for custom fitting to the user's needs, and to prevent unraveling.

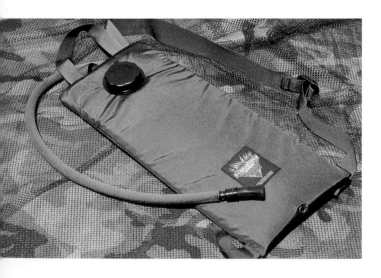

HydraStorm is an integrated hydration system offered by BlackHawk Industries. The company's literature states that its product is "designed and manufactured by operators, for operators!" An operator will typically attach two 2-pound canteens to his pistol belt, but these can be awkward to carry and access. Wearing the HydraStorm on his back, the operator will find the bite valve readily available while on the move, without the need to fumble around for a canteen and canteen cover.

This operator has snaked the drinking tube from his CamelBak hydration bladder through an accessory patch attached to his vest. This position allows him quick access to his water without stopping to pull a canteen. The vest is an Omega Tactical Vest-1 manufactured by BlackHawk Industries. It features six adjustable pouches that will accommodate two 30-round M4 magazines per pouch.

The CamelBak hydration system is a plastic water bladder connected to a length of hose. It fits into an insulated bag that can be strapped on the carrier's back or attached to a rucksack. The hose is positioned close to the wearer's shoulder strap to eliminate snagging on obstacles. Since the water does not slosh, the system is silent.

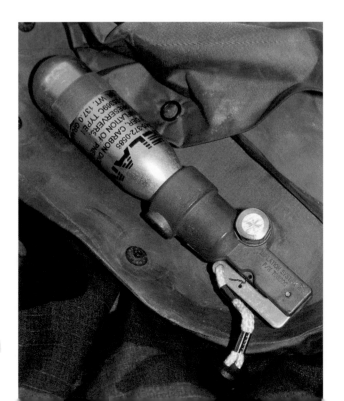

Still in use to day is the old UDT vest, which is inflated by a CO_2 cartridge. It also has a back-up manual inflation tube.

Left: **Close-up view of the CO_2 cartridge.**

105

This photo shows an M9 Beretta in a tactical holster. Most operators opt to carry their side arm in what is called a drop-down holster. Attaching to the pistol belt with an extension hanger places the holster just above the knee. The benefit of this style of holster is that it allows greater stability and ease of access in combat situations. During missions, operators will tend to carry the pistol either on a drop-down holster attached to their leg, or attached to an assault vest. Carrying the pistol on the leg allows quick access, but it can flop around and sometimes catch on ledges or edges. Wearing the pistol on the vest reverses these concerns, but then it can become more difficult to access. Defense Visual Image Center

The 6004 tactical holster from Safariland is built for comfort as well as performance. The holster features a rotating closure that allows the operator to carry the weapon at condition 0, which means the weapon is loaded and cocked, a round is in the chamber, and the safety is off. The rotating strap is moved out of the way by pressing down on the release catch and pushing the strap forward. The holster uses a thermal-molded plastic, which protects the pistol from scratches and dents in a tactical environment. The 6004 leg shroud and the double leg straps make the holster comfortable as well as stable for use in a tactical situation.

While the teams are equipped with the most lethal weaponry, they also employ low-tech equipment. Knee pads provide protection when it's time to "hit the deck," or rapidly navigate through a building. These hard plastic outers are foam-lined and have open slots in the back to allow extra padding. Elbow pads are often employed as well. U.S. Navy

As with other equipment, SEALs are given a wide latitude in eye protection. These tactical goggles (left) are the Bolle Commando model, a multi-purpose goggle that provides protection from fragments, sand, dust, etc. The goggles feature a foamless system that allows them to seal to the operator's face. Military free-fall goggles (center) provide protection from the wind during HALO and helicopter operations. And the Bolle Attacker goggle (right) is another choice for tactical use. Favored in many counterterrorist units, they can also be found in the SEAL kit bags. The Attacker goggles feature foam that molds to the operator's face.

When the need for a goggle system arises, the SEALs may turn to the WileyX SG-1 Ballistic goggles. This system can be configured as a goggle with strap or earpieces for a more traditional sunglass configuration. It also comes with shaded and clear lenses, which are interchangeable, depending on the wearer's needs against sun, wind, and dust. Shown in the center is the WileyX Romer II fitted with light rust lenses.

Taking the IR square a step further, this operator is wearing an infrared reflective American flag. Attached with Velcro, this flag seen in ambient light appears as an OD/Black national ensign. When illuminated with an IR light, it will glow with a bright radiance.

United States flag, as seen under IR light.

Left: **A specially designed infrared (IR) reflective material is affixed to this operator's BDU pocket. This 1-inch by 1-inch GloTape resembles black duct tape both in look and texture, but when the square is illuminated with an IR source, a bright reflection can be seen through a night-vision device at exceptionally long distances. The use of this tape is to provide an identification of operators, vehicles, and equipment in a covert environment so as to avoid fratricide among friendly forces.**

NIGHT-VISION EQUIPMENT

The AN/PVS-7 is a single-tube night-vision goggle (NVG), Generation III/Omni IV image intensifier utilizing prisms and lenses to provide the operator user with simulated binocular vision. The AN/PVS-7 contains a high light-level protection circuit in a passive, self-contained image intensifier device that amplifies existing ambient light to provide the operator a means of conducting night operations.

The AN/PVS-14 night-vision monocular may be worn on an assembly mounted on the U.S. military's standard PAGST Kevlar combat helmet, or it can be mounted directly on the operator's weapon. The AN/PVS-14 incorporates adjustments, front and back, and flip-up/flip-down capability. An optional 3-power focal magnifier lens assembly is designed to temporarily attach to the objective lens for long-range viewing. Similar to the AN/PVS-7 NVG, an optional magnetic compass module can be attached to the AN/PVS-14, providing the easily read magnetic heading in the field of view.

The AN/PVS-21 low-profile night-vision goggles were designed to meet the needs of stealth and aggressive night-vision operations. The AN/PVS-21 LP/NVG features three unique characteristics— "folded optics;" an innovative see-through capability; and a built-in heads-up display (HUDO)—that provide the operator with matchless versatility.

The AN/PVS-7 is a lightweight, high-performance passive third-generation image-intensifier system. Using these night-vision goggles (NVG) turns the night into day. The NVG unit is a self-contained night-vision system containing one binocular unit consisting of an objective lens assembly, an image-intensifier tube, a housing assembly, and a binocular eyepiece assembly. The AN/PVS-7 can be worn on a head mounting assembly around the operator's neck for instant use, or stashed away in the assault vest. To aid in close-proximity viewing, the NVG has an infrared (IR) light source that provides illumination. It is shown here attached to a side-cut Pro-tec helmet.

AN/PVS-14, manufactured by ITT, is the optimum night-vision monocular for special applications. It can be hand held, mounted on a facemask or helmet, or attached to the RIS/RAS of a weapon. The user can operate with it on one eye and maintain night vision in the other eye.

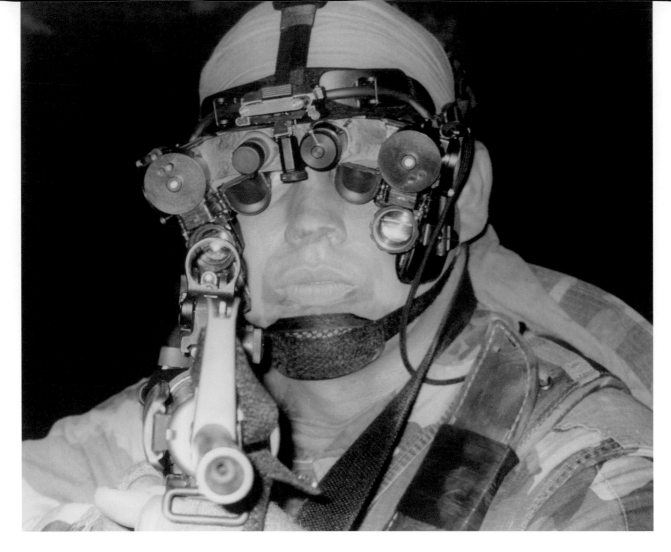

The AN/PVS-21 Low-Profile/Night-Vision Goggle uses a patented folded optical system for a low-profile NVG with see-through capability. The two image intensifier tubes are positioned vertically rather than horizontally, and the two objective lenses are situated at cheek level on each side of the face. This placement provides a low center of gravity and thus eliminates neck fatigue and reduces the possibility of entangling the goggles with other objects. The AN/PVS-21 is a rugged, self-contained device that operates on one AA battery. Specialized Technical Services

The AN/PVS-21 can be mounted on numerous helmet systems including Pro-tec, Kevlar, and aviation helmets, as well as on a special harness for use without headgear. The unit is waterproof to one atmosphere and has a low profile to allow aggressive movement, even in rough terrain.

The AN/PVS-21 can also be fitted with a miniature heads-up display (HUD) that can display real-time information such as GPS coordinates, compass bearings, and other alphanumeric imagery. Specialized Technical Services

RADIOS

Communications is the lifeline of any SEAL team on a mission. For long-range communications, the AN/PRC-117F covers the entire 30- to 512-MHz frequency range while offering embedded COMSEC, and Havequick I/II ECCM capabilities. This advanced-software reprogrammable digital radio supports continuous operation across the 90- to 420-MHz band, providing 20 W FM and 10 W AM transmit power with Havequick I/II capability (or 10 W FM in other frequency ranges). The radio supports both DS-101 and DS-102 fill interfaces and all common fill devices for Havequick Word-of-Day (WOD) and encryption key information. The devices support the Department of Defense requirement for a lightweight, secure, network-capable, multi-band, multi-mission, anti-jam, voice/imagery/data communication capability in a single package.

Motorola has been providing communication gear for the U.S. Special Operations community for decades, from suitcase SATCOMs to secure personalized radios. The Motorola Company's support in making operations successful is paramount in the industry. Here we present one of their latest contributions, the ASTRO SABER.

The AN/PRC-117F has a removable keypad with which the RTO can control the radio's parameters while it is being carried on his back. The radio weighs 15.9 pounds with batteries and is 3.2 inches high by 10.5 inches wide by 13.5 inches deep. It offers an embedded GPS interface capability that will transmit the user's coordinate when the operator keys the handset.

The multi-band AN/PRC-117F operates in VHF AM and FM, UHF AM, and UHF DAMA SATCOM. DAMA (Demand Assigned Multiple Access) permits several hundred users to share one narrowband SATCOM channel based on need or demand. It is a voice/data unit with embedded crypto, SATCOM, and ECCM capabilities.

ASTRO SABER digital technology delivers consistent audio quality throughout the operator's coverage area. This technology provides enhanced signaling and control, greater spectral efficiency, and a full range of encryption capabilities. It is a fully functional, digital portable radio with the flexibility to work in both digital and analog environments. Individual users can custom program commonly used or critical features on a radio-by-radio basis through programmable buttons and soft-key access. A ruggedized version is available for use in demanding environments such as heat, vapor, or salt water.

For tactical intra-team communications, the SEALs will be issued the new multi-band inter/intra team radios, which provide communications on user-selected frequency from 30 to 512 MHz utilizing a single hand-held radio. The new radio provides up to 5 watts in VHF/FM, VHF/AM, UHF/AM, UHF/FM(LOS) for ground-to-ground and air-to-ground connectivity. Weighing only 31 ounces, there are two versions, immersable to 6 feet and to 66 feet. The units incorporate communications security (COMSEC) for full digital voice and data operations.

The "Ruggedized" ASTRO SABER Digital Radio from Motorola is compatible with a full array of Motorola's current analog systems, including Conventional STAT-Alert, SECURENET systems, SMARTNET Type II, and Smart Zone trunked systems digital technology. It delivers consistent voice quality throughout the operator's coverage area, enhanced signaling and control, greater spectral efficiency, and improved secure communications. Digital solutions are available in VHF, UHF, and 800 MHz frequencies for both conventional and trunked applications with enhanced encryption, COMSEC US Type 1.

Thale's multi-band inter/intra team radio (MBITR) is a powerful tactical handheld radio designed for the U.S. Special Operations Command. Designated the AN/PRC-148, it provides a secure voice and digital-data radio with exceptional versatility, ruggedness, and reliability. The immersible unit weighs less than 2 pounds and includes a keypad, graphics display, and built-in speaker-microphone. The MBITR has embedded Type 1 COMSEC for both voice and data traffic.

By joining the MBITR and the PLGR, SEALs can transmit the GPS coordinates seamlessly and directly to their command using a secure communications link.

Thales Communication Multiband Inter/Intra Team Radio (MBITR) is a powerful tactical hand-held radio designed for the U.S. Special Operations Command. The MBITR more than meets the tough SOCOM requirements and provides a secure voice and digital-data radio with exceptional versatility, ruggedness, and reliability.

The immersable unit weighs less than 2 pounds and includes a keypad, graphics display, and built-in speaker-microphone. Typical of the advanced designs produced by Thales, MBITR utilizes digital-signal processing and flash memory to support functions traditionally performed by discrete hardware in other manufacturers' equipment. The power output is up to 5 watts over the 30- to 512-MHz frequency band. The MBITR has embedded Type 1 COMSEC for voice and data traffic.

The Rockwell Precision Lightweight GPS Receiver 96 (PLGR+96, or "Plugger") is sealed for operations in all environments. It will continuously compute accurate position coordinates, elevation, speed, and time data from up to five Navstar GPS satellites' transmitted signals.

Shown here are a Silva Ranger compass (left) and an issued GI compass (right). The lensatic compass has been used by the military for decades. The self-luminous tritium light sources provide readability in total darkness.

GLOBAL POSITIONING SYSTEM

While all SOF operators excel in land navigation using the standard-issue lensetic compass, it is equally important for the teams to be able to benefit from pinpoint accuracy when conducting direct action missions through the desert, or across the frozen tundra in the middle of the night. Operators need to know the position of a terrorist's hideout, a radar station, or perhaps a WMD cache when reporting in to headquarters. For such instances, they will utilize the world-wide global positioning system (GPS).

The global positioning system is a collection of satellites that orbit the earth twice a day, transmitting precise time, latitude, longitude, and altitude information. Using a GPS receiver, a special-operations team can ascertain its exact location anywhere on earth.

For underwater infiltration, the SEALs use RJE International's combat swim board for navigation. The board incorporates an underwater compass, a depth gauge, and underwater chronograph mounted to a light-weight plastic board with handles for ease of use.

Global Positioning System (GPS)

Developed by the U.S. Department of Defense in the early 1970s to provide a continuous, world-wide positioning and navigational system for U.S. military forces around the globe, the GPS complete constellation, as it is referred to, consists of 24 satellites orbiting approximately 12,000 miles above the Earth. These 22 active and 2 reserve satellites provide data 24 hours a day for 2D and 3D positioning anywhere on the planet. Each satellite constantly broadcasts precise time and location data to troops using a GPS receiver.

By measuring the time interval of the transmission and the receipt of the satellite signal, the GPS receiver calculates the distance between itself and each satellite. Using the distance measurements of at least three satellites in an algorithmic computation, the GPS receiver provides the precise location. Using a special encryption signal results in the Precise Positioning Service (PPS) used by the military. A second signal, called Standard Positioning Service (SPS), is available for civilian and commercial use.

The current GPS unit is the Rockwell PSN-11 Precise Lightweight GPS Receiver 96 (PLGR+96, or "Plugger"). The PLGR+96 is the most advanced version of the U.S. Department of Defense hand-held GPS unit. It addresses the increasingly demanding requirements of the SEALs and all the other U.S. Special Operations forces.

Secure (Y-code) Differential GPS (SDGPS) allows the user to accept differential correction without zeroing the unit. Differential accuracy can be less than one meter. Other features of the "Plugger" include: wide-area GPS enhancement (WAGE), for autonomous positioning accuracy to 4 meters; jammer direction finding; targeting interface with laser range-finder; remote display terminal capability; and advanced user interface features.

Weighing in at a mere 2.7 pounds (with batteries installed), the GPS unit is easily stowed in the rucksack or even in a pocket of an assault vest of the SEAL operators. In addition to hand-held operation the PLGR+96 unit can be installed on various vehicles and airborne platforms.

For missions that require operators to infiltrate underwater, the miniature underwater global positioning system receiver (MUGR) provides the team with position and navigational information needed for infil/exfil, fire support, direct action, and target location. This small device weighs a mere 1.2 pounds. Once the unit acquires the satellite fix, the waterproof MUGR can be taken to a depth of 33 feet. Alternately, the unit works underwater by utilizing the optional floating antenna.

SPECIAL OPERATION FORCES— LASER ACQUISITION MARKER

A Special Operations forces–laser acquisition marker (SOFLAM) is used in a direct-action mission for the direction of terminal-guided ordnance (TGO), a technique referred to as "lasing the target." When it absolutely, positively, has to be destroyed, a team on the ground links up with a fast mover's smart bomb in the air. This typically results in rubble centered on a smoking bomb crater. The newly issued SOFLAM is lighter and more compact than the current laser marker in service with the U.S. military. It provides the operators with the capability to locate and designate critical enemy targets for destruction via laser-guided ordnance. It can be used in daylight or with attached night-vision optics.

The AN/PEQ-1A can be implemented as part of a sophisticated, digitized fire-control system with thermal or image-intensified sights.

AN/PEQ-1A SOFLAM

Northop-Grumman SOFLAM officially designated ground laser target designator (GLTD II) is a compact, lightweight, portable laser-target designator and rangefinder. It exports range data and imports azimuth

and elevation via an RS422 link. It is designed to enable special-operations forces to direct such laser-guided smart weapons as Paveway bombs, Hellfire missiles, and Copperhead munitions.

The Phoenix IR transmitter, weighing a mere 2 ounces, is a pocket-size, user-programmable on/off IR strobe beacon designed for personal combat identification (CID). It is invisible to the naked eye, but when observed through night-vision goggles it can be seen up to 20 miles away. A 9-volt battery, lightweight and easy to use, powers the transmitter. The other unit contains two protruding pins that allow the unit to be programmed with a varying series of patterns.

While SEAL teams are equipped with the latest high-tech equipment, the venerable smoke grenade still has a place in the rucksacks and assault vests of these elite troopers. It is not unusual to find a smoke grenade or two attached to a SEAL's LBE or assault vest for signaling positions or marking a helicopter landing zone for pickup. Seen here is an assortment of M18 colored-smoke grenades in violet, yellow, and green (red is also available). The grenade produces a cloud of colored smoke for 50 to 90 seconds.

Seen here are two MS-2000(M) strobe lights. This omni-directional white light is equivalent to 250,000 lumens. The light on the left has the IR (infrared) shield in place, which is visible only with night-vision goggles. The unit on the right has the cover off. The strobe also features a blue filter, which differentiates the signal of the strobe from ground fire. The strobe is useful to facilitate close air support, combat search-and-rescue operations, and other ground-to-air signaling. Operators can affix the lights to their helmets when performing HALO/HAHO jumps to identify team members.

Members of a SEAL team practice ship-board insertion and exfiltration techniques. The SEALs fast-roped onto U.S. Merchant Marine Vessel PFC *Obergon* from an MH-53 Pave Low helicopter of the U.S. Air Force Special Operations Command's 20th Special Operations Squadron. After fast-roping onto the ship, the SEALs provide cover for each other during a search-and-seizure exercise. U.S. Navy

When the SEALs come knocking, it is not always with breaching charges; sometimes they utilize manual methods. These dynamic-entry tools from BlackHawk Industries are, clockwise, a Special Operations Hallagan Tool, Electra Shield Bolt Master, and Thunder sledge. All of the tools are non-conducting to protect the operator from electric shock. The Hallagan Tool weighs 5.75 pounds and is 24 inches in length. With a forked end and a wedge at the other end, it provides maximum leverage. It is a very effective entry tool. The bolt cutter is also 24 inches long, weighs 5.25 pounds, and features a .375-inch jaw opening. The advanced polymer handle is nonconductive to 100,000 volts. The sledge weighs in at 6.5 pounds and is 21 inches long. The handle is made of advanced polymer with a non-slip coating that prevents the tool from absorbing shards of glass during operations.

The SOFLAM uses the pulse-repetition frequency (PRF) which can either be set to NATO STANAG (Standards and Agreements, as established by NATO) Band I or II, or is programmable. PRF is the number of pulses per second transmitted by a laser.

A common practice among many of the special operations forces is the attachment of a strobe pouch to the BDU. This allows the operator to keep his strobe with his first-line gear. In the event he has to abandon all other equipment, such as LBE or vest, he will still have a means for signaling friendly forces.

Author's Note

The Future, From the Sea and Beyond

On September 20, 2001, nine days after the terrorist attack on America, President George W. Bush addressed a joint session of Congress. During his speech, he pointed at the members of the Joint Chiefs of Staff and gave them their directive, "Be Ready." Chief of Naval Operations Admiral Vern Clark later commented, "[We] need to give the Commander-in-Chief the options he needs, when he needs it."

The Cold War approach of massing troops along European tree lines has been replaced with the surgical strikes of smaller, more precise actions. Today's warfare requires a warrior capable of thinking outside the box, an operator who evolves every day. The GWOT is a 24/7 mission, and the Navy SEALs have stood up to the task at hand. Since the inception of Operation Enduring Freedom, SEALs have been chosen for a wide assortment of missions: direct-action and special-reconnaissance operations in the mountains of Afghanistan, maritime operations in the Arabian Gulf, the rescue of a young Army private in Iraq, and countless other missions that may never come to light.

On February 12, 2002, Secretary of the Navy Gordon England stated before the Senate Armed Service Committee, "[America's] naval forces have demonstrated the reach of their lethal power deep into the enemy heartland. Operating beyond the traditional littoral, we have destroyed the enemy in areas that they previously considered sanctuaries."

Today's Navy SEALs, steeped in the heritage of those naked warriors who went before, stand ready to meet that challenge. Their mission is to attack with speed, agility, and precision at the heart of those who threaten our liberties and freedom. Attacked with such intensity, no enemy would ever seek a rematch.

Today's Naval Special Warfare operators accomplish their stealth infiltration via nuclear submarine and SDVs. Tomorrow these methods will evolve into stealth surface ships as the platform for insertion. Military capability in the future may focus on sea basing, which will permit the SEALs to initiate sustainable operations as well as establish a maritime presence around the globe. From these bases of operation, Naval Special Warfare will project a credible, persistent combat power over the horizon, well off of any hostile shore, from international waters.

Without question, Navy SEALs are armed and equipped with the latest and best weaponry and high-tech gear. It does not matter if intelligence comes from an orbiting UAV or local HUMINT; SEALs are prepared to engage at a moment's notice. Regardless of the weapon or technology he employs, it is the operator in the arena of combat who wins the battle. Whether he is armed with an assault rifle or a merely a Ka-Bar, he will prosecute his mission no matter what the odds. These are the warriors of the U.S. Navy SEALs, to whom "failure is not an option" and "The Only Easy Day Was Yesterday."

Antiterrorism (AT):
Defensive measures used to reduce the vulnerability of individuals and property to terrorism.

Clandestine operation:
Activities sponsored or conducted by governmental departments or agencies in such a way as to assure secrecy or concealment. (This differs from covert operations in that emphasis is placed upon concealment of the operation rather than on concealment of the sponsor's identity.) In Special Operations, an activity may be both covert and clandestine, and it may focus equally on operational considerations and intelligence-related activities.

Close air support (CAS):
Air action against hostile targets that are in close proximity to friendly ground forces and which require detailed integration of each air mission with the fire and movement of those ground forces.

Counterproliferation:
Activities taken to counter the spread of dangerous military capabilities, allied technologies, and/or knowhow, especially weapons of mass destruction and ballistic missile delivery systems.

Counterterrorism (CT):
Offensive measures taken to prevent, deter, and respond to terrorism.

Covert operations:
Operations that are planned and executed so as to conceal the identity of or permit plausible denial by the sponsor.

Crisis:
An incident or situation involving a threat to the United States, its territories, citizens, military forces, and possessions or vital interests that develops rapidly and creates a condition of such diplomatic, economic, political, or military importance that commitment of U.S. military forces and resources is contemplated to achieve national objectives.

Direct action mission:
In special operations, a specified act involving operations of an overt, covert, clandestine, or low-visibility nature conducted primarily by a sponsoring power's special operations forces in hostile or denied areas.

Exfiltration (Exfil):
The removal of personnel or units from areas under enemy control.

Infiltration (Infil):
The movement through or into an area or territory occupied by either friendly or enemy troops or organizations. The movement is made, either by small groups or by individuals, at extended or irregular intervals. When used in connection with the enemy, it implies that contact is avoided.

Insurgency:
An organized movement aimed at the overthrow of a constituted government through the use of subversion and armed conflict.

Internal defense:
The full range of measures taken by a government to free and protect its society from subversion, lawlessness, and insurgency.

Interoperability:
The ability of systems, units, or forces to provide services to and accept services from other systems, units, or forces, and use of the services so exchanged to enable them to operate effectively together.

Low-intensity conflict:
Political-military confrontation between contending states or groups below conventional war and above routine, peaceful competition among states. It frequently involves protracted struggles of competing principles and ideologies. Low-intensity conflict ranges from subversion to the use of limited armed force. It is waged by a combination of means employing political, economic, informational, and military instruments. Low-intensity conflicts are often localized, generally in the Third World, but contain regional and global security implications.

National Command Authorities (NCA):
The President and the Secretary of Defense together, or their duly deputized alternates or successors. The term signifies Constitutional authority to direct the Armed Forces in their execution of military action. The President is the only Commander-in-Chief (CinC).

Objectives:
Specific actions to be achieved in a specified time period. Accomplishment will indicate progress toward achieving the goals.

Operator:
See Shooter.

Psychological operations (PsyOps):
Planned operations to convey selected information and indicators to foreign audiences in order to influence their emotions, motives, objective reasoning, and ultimately the behavior of foreign governments, organizations, groups, and individuals. The purpose of psychological operations is to induce or reinforce foreign attitudes and behavior favorable to the originator's objectives.

Shooter:
A trooper belonging to a Special Operations forces unit (e.g., U.S. Army Rangers, U.S. Army Special Forces, Delta, Marine Force Recon, U.S. Navy SEALs, Special Air Service (SAS))

Special reconnaissance:
Reconnaissance and surveillance actions conducted by special-operations forces to obtain or verify, by visual observation or other collection methods, information concerning the capabilities, intentions, and activities of an actual or potential enemy, or to secure data concerning the meteorological, hydrographic, or geographic characteristics of a particular area. It includes target acquisition, area assessment, and post-strike reconnaissance.

ACRONYMS & ABBREVIATIONS

AFSOC	Air Force Special Operations Command
ASDS	Advanced SEAL Delivery System
AT4	Shoulder-fired, disposable antitank weapon
CAC	Coastal assault craft
CAG	Combat application group
CAS	Close air support
CSAR	Combat search-and-rescue
COTS	Commercial off-the-shelf
CT	Counterterrorism
CQB	Close-quarters battle
CRE	Close-range engagement
DA	Direct action
DEVGRU	Development group
DOD	Department of Defense
DZ	Drop zone
E&R	Evasion and recovery
FRIS	Fast-rope insertion system

GPS	Global positioning system
HAHO	High-altitude, high opening
HALO	High-altitude, low opening
HE	High explosives
HUMINT	Human intelligence
JSOC	Joint Special Operations Command
LBE	Load-bearing equipment
LBV	Load-bearing vest
LZ	Landing zone
MOUT	Military operations in urban terrain
MST	Mobile support team
NOD	Night optical device
NVG	Night-vision goggles
PBL	Patrol boat, light
RAS	Rail attachment system
RIS	Rail interface system
SEAL	SEa, Air, Land (U.S. Navy Special Operations forces)
SAR	Search-and-rescue
SAS	Special Air Service (U.K. or Australia)
SBS	Special Boat Squadron (U.K.)
SF	Special Forces (U.S. Army)
SOCOM	Special Operations Command
SOCR	Special operations craft, riverine
SOF	Special Operations forces
SOFLAM	Special Operations forces laser acquisition
SOPMOD	Special Operations peculiar modifications
SR	Special reconnaissance
WMD	Weapons of mass destruction

Index

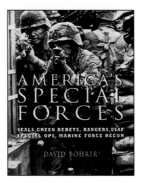
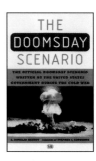

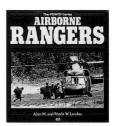